Rails Through Lakeland

Volume 1

The beauty of the CKPR: on Whit Monday 1963 a Carlisle-Keswick train approaches Keswick hauled by a pair of Ivatt Class '2MT' 2-6-0s. *Stephen Crook*

Rails Through Lakeland

An illustrated history of the Workington-Cockermouth-Keswick-Penrith Railway, 1847-1972

Volume 1
The line described

Harold D. Bowtell

· RAILWAY HERITAGE ·
from
The NOSTALGIA Collection

First published in a single volume as *Rails Through Lakeland* in June 1989
Reprinted June 1991
Volume 1 of a two-volume paperback edition first published April 1999

British Library Cataloguing in Publication Data

A catalogue record for this book is available from the British Library.

ISBN 1 85794 066 0

Silver Link Publishing Ltd
The Trundle
Ringstead Road
Great Addington
Kettering
Northants
NN14 4BW

Tel/Fax: 01536 330588
email: sales@slinkp-p.demon.co.uk

Printed and bound in Great Britain

Abbreviations

C&WJnR	Cleator & Workington Junction Railway
C&WR	Cockermouth & Workington Railway
CKPR	Cockermouth, Keswick & Penrith Railway
LMS	London Midland & Scottish Railway
LNWR	London & North Western Railway
M&CR	Maryport & Carlisle Railway
NER	North Eastern Railway
S&DR	Stockton & Darlington Railway
WC&ER	Whitehaven, Cleator & Egremont Railway
wef	with effect from
WJnR	Whitehaven Junction Railway

Contents

On 7 August 1950 '18-inch goods' 0-6-0 No 58389 is seen standing in the Up platform at Threlkeld with the 11.50am ex-Workington train. This is the eastern end of the station; note the distinctive and most unusual signal box at the western end of the island platform buildings. *E. S. Russell*

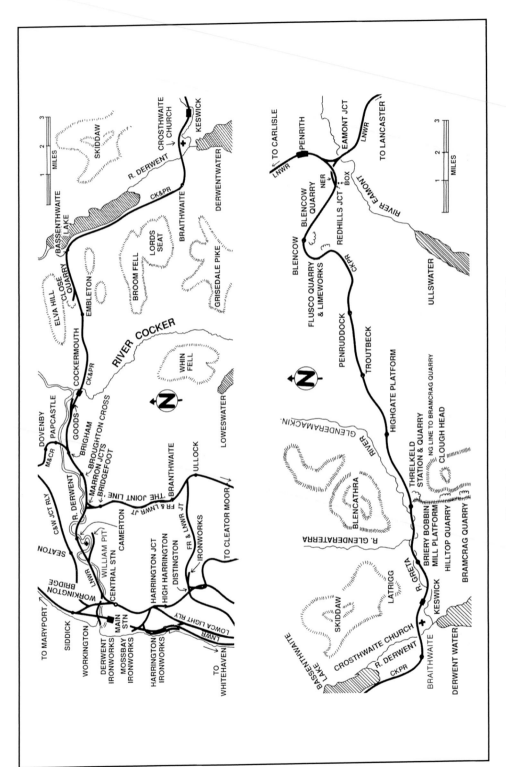

The Workington-Cockermouth-Keswick-Penrith Railway

Author's Preface

Every railway has its own unique character. This is created not only by impressive features, such as a Kilsby Tunnel, bridges by Brunel, or engineering works of the kind found between Settle and Carlisle. Character is the sum of a complex recipe: the country and the towns, and the traffics conveyed, all contribute – but above all it is the people who create character. The families and folk who ran the Keswick line were quietly dedicated and I have sought to give them a little more individual attention than is usually possible in histories of 'grander' railways. An effort is also made to indicate how the local company Directors and also those nominated by the London & North Western Railway (LNWR) and North Eastern Railway (NER) were caring figures in the railway and the communities it served.

Other notables from the earlier years who come into the story include William Wordsworth and his son, the Reverend John Wordsworth, and, from the middle period, Canon Rawnsley of Crosthwaite (Keswick) and the National Trust. The Canon was at Carlisle Cathedral when he received a telegram from the Editor of the *Daily News* telling of the death of Scott of the Antarctic – and he composed a suitable sonnet while returning to Keswick by train that afternoon. It was duly carried by the CKPR, LNWR and the Post Office in time to be published in the newspaper in London the next day.

Rather less confidence was shown by the writer of the message on a picture postcard from Lakeland: 'I will come (to Manchester) tomorrow by the train leaving Keswick at 3.50. The trains on this line are very late ... all the trains on this line are very late today, they are not particular about time on this line. It is very wet tonight.' Nevertheless, the Post Office (with the Railways' assistance) was relied on to deliver this card, postmarked at Keswick at 7.00am on 16 August 1906, to a Manchester suburban address the same afternoon, and doubtless did so.

Rural aspects also come through. There is William Boyd's memory of his schooldays trip from Edinburgh to Keswick in August 1920. Leaving Penrith, a swishing sound not evident on the 'Caley' or Lancaster & Carlisle main lines was evident – and it proved to be that of the CKPR train passing through the long grass! Again, in the 1930s, a certain station master became cross with engine drivers who repeatedly stopped to pick mushrooms in the fields near his station. So he picked them himself and substituted empty eggshells; after a few abortive halts, the drivers had their suspicions, but desisted.

Concerning the setting of the railway and touching on just one aspect, H. H. Symonds (*Walking in the Lake District*, 1933) wrote '... Saddleback ... many look at it from carriage windows, as the train from Penrith comes first in sight of it at Penruddock, then warms to it by Troutbeck, and at last is smothered under the glory of it all the way to Threlkeld and on into the woods and cuttings towards Keswick. These are six miles of "parly third" which leave the World's Best Permanent Way, the Royal Scot, the thunders of Shap Summit, nowhere.'

The general map in two overlapping sections (opposite) sets the route of our railway (and its junctions and stations) in perspective amid the rivers, lakes and mountains. Original siding diagrams of 1874 and 1915-17 are reproduced (with a little extraneous detail removed, for clarity) to expand details of the once industrial western end of the route. Where available in suitable form, LMS engineering and estate department plans of the 1930s form the basis of station plans, notably depicting Cockermouth and Keswick stations, but also part of Brigham, Penruddock and Blencow. Cockermouth's elongated junction and goods yard, and plans of the station layouts at Bassenthwaite Lake and Troutbeck, are also provided. Richard Foster has made available his reconstruction, basically illustrating the 1920s-1930s period, of Threlkeld, which provides an emphasis on signalling, and is complemented by his architectural presentation and various photographs.

The reader may ask why the line is not described westward, from Penrith to Workington? This is because the railway began life in the west, between Workington and Cockermouth (in 1847), and following its opening throughout in 1864-65 the emphasis was on working the coal pits in the west and carrying coke from Durham to West Cumberland's ironworks. The pattern became, in time, one of primarily passenger and tourist travel, chiefly on the Keswick section, and the last part to operate (until 1972) was between Keswick and Penrith. The story is therefore taken from Workington to Cockermouth, to Keswick and finally to Penrith.

Regrettably, the railway is no more. Why did it disappear? The study in this work of the multitude of bridges – mainly designed in the first place by (Sir) Thomas Bouch – hints at one of the economic reasons. Then there is the total disappearance of the basic traffic in coke westward, along with the decline of the collieries and shipment of their output; after all, these were the traffics that the railway was built to carry. Also, by the early 1960s there was pressure by the Ministry of Transport to build a virtually new road between Penrith and West Cumberland. There was pressure too to provide such a link as impetus to the establishment of a bus-building factory near Workington. For many miles, the railway's route provided a tempting right of way, which in the event was taken over for long stretches and greatly widened for the new road. A parallel local bus service survived the railway but, from November 1985, this all but disappeared between Penrith and Keswick, with only two daily workings each way advertised.

The railway is long gone, but there are still many reminders of its presence to be viewed and explored. I hope that this account, in words, pictures and plans, will enable the residents of Lakeland, railway enthusiasts and historians and many other visitors to locate and interpret the scenes and surviving structures.

Harold D. Bowtell,
Kendal, Westmorland, 1989

1. Setting the scene

The Cockermouth & Workington Railway

Authorised by an initial Act of 23 July 1845, this essentially single-track link of some 8½ miles extended from a terminal station at the west end of Cockermouth to Workington Harbour. It was designed primarily to carry coals from pits (to be connected to it) for shipment from Workington. Opening for all traffic was on 28 April 1847. From a convergence at Derwent Junction with the Whitehaven Junction Railway (WJnR), the C&WR's passenger train – the Company had an engine and carriages for but a single train – crossed the river and ran south to reach the WJnR's nearly new, but scarcely grandiose, Workington station. This was remote from the town (to eastward) and the sea (to the west). Workington was at this time newly connected with Carlisle, following completion of the Maryport & Carlisle Railway (M&CR) on 10 February 1845, and

A delightful and characteristic scene looking west at Cockermouth in the early 1900s. The permanent way lengthmen take a break from their work as an unidentified LNWR 'Cauliflower' 0-6-0 coasts into the platform with a four-coach Up passenger service, for which a group of smartly attired ladies and gentlemen are waiting, outside the station's refreshment room. The hot summer weather is clearly apparent: note the ladies' sunhats and the gents' straw 'boaters'! On the right, cattle wagons (with their lower planking 'limed' to prevent the spread of disease) are awaiting their next turn of duty, probably in connection with Cockermouth's Monday market. *The Sankey Collection*

with the WJnR, Maryport-Workington (from 19 January 1846), which was extended from Workington to Whitehaven Bransty on 19 March 1847. Not until 1857 was there a through connection southwards (via the coastal line) to Carnforth and thereby the London & North Western Railway's Anglo-Scottish main line from Euston to Scotland.

The C&WR's 19 years of independence were conducted with surprisingly little cognisance of its coastal neighbours – and it never persevered with, or supported, the early project for an extension eastward, following the northern shore of Bassenthwaite Lake, to Keswick.

The Cockermouth, Keswick & Penrith Railway

The Cockermouth, Keswick & Penrith Railway (CKPR) was constituted under an Act of Parliament of 1 August 1861, with authorised capital of £200,000, accompanied by the authority to raise £66,000 by loans; a modest increase in capital was made in 1876-77. The undertaking was a more substantial affair, in both aims and achievement, than the purely local C&WR. What the CKPR lacked in direct association with industry, it compensated for in its cross-country linkage of industrial interests, and its superb setting in northern Lakeland. Construction was put in hand, leading to the opening of its entire route – some 31 miles – for mineral traffic on 4 November 1864 and subsequently to passengers on 2 January 1865.

In 1861, and until 1866, the CKPR was financially independent of its existing western neighbour, the C&WR – and, in a sense, this independence continued until the railway Grouping of 1923. However, the linking at Cockermouth of the existing C&WR and the projected CKPR was an essential feature of the Keswick Company's scheme, as only by this means could its powerful friends to the east be enabled to operate important end-to-end through traffics. The completion of arrangements with the London & North Western Railway and the Stockton & Darlington Railway (soon to become part of the North Eastern Railway) was a priority for

The splendid setting of the Penrith-Workington route is amply illustrated by this view from Latrigg, circa 1895-96. Keswick station and the impressive hotel are visible in the foreground, backed to southward by the town, Derwentwater and the mountains of central Lakeland. *Author's collection*

the Keswick Board. This would associate it with two railways that served a major part of British industry and which, through the ensuing 60 years, clearly appreciated the extent of their mutual interests.

Negotiations during February-September 1862 produced agreements with the LNWR, as also with the S&DR, confirmed and signed in each case. The CKPR Act of 29 June 1863 followed, each of the other Companies being allowed to subscribe £25,000 to the CKPR. The LNWR was to operate all passenger and goods trains on the CKPR line and was to receive 33⅓% (increased in 1889 to 35%) of the relevant receipts. The NER was to operate mineral trains and receive 35% of receipts from minerals. The Keswick Company was thereby relieved of the need to provide rolling-stock or guards for commercial traffic. Locomotive power and engine crews were likewise to be the responsibility of the larger Companies.

A potential community of interest between the giant LNWR, with headquarters at Euston, and the small Companies of West Cumberland (C&WR and WJnR) was apparent. During 1864 and 1865 both the LNWR and the CKPR, acting independently, were in touch with the C&WR concerning

prospects for traffic working, or merger. Also, the CKPR secured some agreement with the LNWR to respect Keswick's relations with the WJnR.

However, hurt feelings followed when it emerged in December 1865 that Mr Fitzsimons, of the LNWR's Lancaster & Carlisle Division, and Mr Stephenson, Traffic Manager of the S&DR, had recently agreed, without reference to Keswick: 1) That the LNWR would convey coal arriving at Penrith from the north for stations on the Keswick line by its goods trains; and 2) That the S&DR would carry pig iron from Workington for stations on the S&DR system by its mineral trains.

The latter point is significant, as it indicates that a west-to-east traffic in pig iron from blast furnaces in West Cumberland was available by the close of 1865.

Nevertheless, the considerable discussions between the LNWR and the CKPR, regarding traffic handling and terms, were amicably concluded and, in May 1866, the 'LNWR, Whitehaven Junction and Cockermouth & Workington Amalgamation Bills' were passed unopposed by the Bill Committee of the House of Commons, and became law as an Act that summer. An interesting provision

No 58362 leaves Penrith with a Workington-bound train on 12 August 1950. The locomotive is an '18-inch goods' of a class familiarly known as 'Cauliflowers', this nickname deriving from the appearance of the LNWR arms sometimes carried in pre-Grouping days. The Eden Valley track is seen to the right of the train, the Down and Up roads of the West Coast Main Line to right again, and the goods yard beyond those. *Neville Fields*

was that the short line to the Lonsdale Dock at Workington was deemed a continuous line of railway for traffic purposes from the WJnR and from the C&WR (the access being at Derwent Junction) and the LNWR was authorised to ship through mineral traffic and pig iron either at Lonsdale Dock or Merchants Quay, Workington. Lonsdale Dock was a new development of 1865, but the Merchants Quay branch and shipment facilities had existed for at least ten years.

The coastal route between Maryport, Derwent Junction, Workington and Whitehaven Bransty, and the line from Cockermouth Goods and Cockermouth Junction to Derwent Junction, thus came to constitute the West Cumberland Lines of the LNWR. There was a degree of local autonomy, but the lines were subservient to the Lancaster & Carlisle Division's Superintendent, based at Lancaster.

Another development peaceably concluded was the extension of the Whitehaven, Cleator & Egremont Railway (WC&ER) northward of Rowrah to join the Cockermouth-Workington line at Marron Junctions, forming a triangular layout with the C&WR route and believed to be opened in January 1866 (for minerals) and April 1866 (for passengers). It was doubled in 1873. In October of 1866 the S&DR/NER-promoted double-track link from Eamont Junction, on the LNWR's Anglo-Scottish main line, to Redhills Junction, on the CKPR just westward of Penrith, was opened. Thus, by the end of 1866, there existed a route for coke traffic from County Durham to Marron Junction and thence to Cleator Moor iron works, also to Workington and those ironworks at Workington and further south, as well as Workington quaysides. These routes were likewise available to any balancing traffic, such as the products of West Cumberland's furnaces, ironstone mines or other industries.

Euston was alive to these matters and some ten years later produced the first LNWR (WCE) Leasing Bill; this became the Act of 26 June 1877, giving the LNWR control of the WC&ER. The CKPR became concerned early in 1878, when a Bill was prepared to authorise leasing of the WC&ER to the

LNWR *and the Furness Railway*; the Keswick Board sought protection against traffic from West Cumberland being diverted from the CKPR to the Furness Railway route. Joint control of the WC&ER by the LNWR and the FR was in fact authorised by an Act of 17 June 1878 and the line was thereafter generally known in Cumberland as the 'the Joint Line'.

The CKPR did not oppose the entirely new railway, to be built from Cleator Moor northward to the town centre of Workington on an inland route broadly parallel with LNWR's coastal route (to its west) and 'the Joint Line' (to its east) – and competitive with both of these. This was the Cleator & Workington Junction Railway (C&WJnR), authorised by an Act of June 1876, and opened from Cleator Moor via Distington to Workington Central station on 1 October 1879. This link became highly significant to the CKPR when its Workington Bridge branch opened on 16 March 1885. This branch provided a direct curve of only 30 chains length, but including a major bridge over the Derwent river, and permitted through running from the CKPR by the C&WR line, Workington Bridge Junction and Cloffocks Junction to the C&WJnR main line (serving potentially Distington and Cleator Moor ironworks) and also the C&WJnR's new branches from Harrington Junction to Moss Bay, Harrington Harbour and Derwent. Note the existence of coastal ironworks at these three sites!

Thus the CKPR-C&WR (LNWR) lines became fully established and developed progressively between 1866 and 1885 as a through route of great industrial significance.

Building the Cockermouth & Workington Railway

The decision to build this railway was taken at a meeting of interested gentlemen, held in the Green Dragon Inn, Workington, on 26 July 1844. A committee was appointed and George Stephenson, whose preliminary advice and estimates had influenced the decision, was to be asked to complete a full survey. The proposed title was 'The Workington and Cockermouth Railway Company', but by

The 'Cauliflower' 0-6-0s were staple motive power on the Keswick road for many years. Here No. 58396 (with Belpaire firebox) pilots another of the same type (but with a round-topped firebox) away from Blencow with a Penrith-Workington train in August 1949. The stock is a mixture of LMS and LNWR designs. *P. B. Whitehouse*

October this was amended to the Cockermouth & Workington Railway. Capital of £70,000 was to be raised, amended in December to £75,000. A survey was carried out by John Dixon, nominally under the direction of George Stephenson; the resulting estimate of £72,000 was close to that of the master himself. John Dixon (1796-1865) of Darlington, was a respected figure, with experience on the construction of the Stockton & Darlington Railway and the Liverpool & Manchester Railway and with recent responsibilities in North East England. Parliamentary plans were deposited in December 1844 and the Act of 23 July 1845 resulted. On 28 June 1845 John Dixon was formally appointed Engineer for the duration of construction and J. C. Fearon was the Assistant Engineer, the latter being resident during the execution of the works.

In July and November 1846 George Stephenson was again consulted when problems arose over acquisition of essential lands at Workington Cloffocks and Merchants Quay, which belonged to the Earl of Lonsdale, of Whitehaven Castle, the most influential landowner in the territories to be traversed by the C&WR. It was November 1845 when the tender of Jacob & William Ritson was accepted as contractors. They were also building the Whitehaven Junction Railway, which was reported to be well advanced in January 1846, and they started on the C&WR works in mid-February 1846, when an adequate part of the requisite lands had been secured.

The route of nearly 9 miles crossed a major river, the Derwent, six times, and subsidiary channels and tributaries were also crossed. Leaving aside the Derwent viaduct at Workington, a responsibility of the WJnR (although to be crossed by C&WR trains), the C&WR had itself to commission 11 bridges of nominal lengths between 50 and 300 feet. Notwithstanding, the single-track route was constructed in only 15 months and opened on

28 April 1847, immediately after inspection by Captain Simmons for the Railway Commissioners.

As early as 15 August 1845, at the first general meeting of the C&WR (soon after its Act had been obtained), there was a hint of possible connection by rail between the Kendal & Windermere Railway (at Windermere) and the C&WR (at Cockermouth). This C&W Extension Railway was independent of the C&WR, which in January 1846 decided that the Extension Railway's section between Cockermouth and Keswick (for which an Act was passed in the ensuing summer) would cost more than £180,000 and would not pay 4%, so they decided against the monetary commitment. The Extension Railway's powers were never exercised.

Building the Cockermouth, Keswick & Penrith Railway

There had been earlier surveys, but pressure for a through cross-country route by way of Keswick developed when a protégé of the Stockton & Darlington Railway secured its Act in 1857 for a railway across the Pennines via Stainmore. Serious surveys via Keswick followed, and that carried out by Thomas Bouch in 1859 produced an estimate not exceeding £200,000; the CKPR's Act of 1861 was based on its findings. Thomas Bouch (1822-1880) was the younger brother of William Bouch, the latter being noted for

A static memorial – one of the two boundary stones still to be seen today in Station Road, Keswick, recalling the Cockermouth, Keswick & Penrith Railway Company, which in 1923 became part of the London Midland & Scottish Railway Company. *Harold D. Bowtell*

both mechanical and civil railway engineering and for water engineering, and in general based at Darlington. Thomas established himself in Edinburgh and was – among many interests – Engineer during construction of the Stainmore line. He was appointed Engineer for construction of the CKPR and in May 1862 the main contracts were let to George Boulton & Son (later & Sons).

As on the C&WR, bridgeworks dominated the engineering of the CKPR. They are of

From Workington to Cockermouth the railway was virtually level, but thereafter the general trend was uphill, with increasingly severe gradients as the summit was approached at Troutbeck, 889 feet above sea level. *Author's collection*

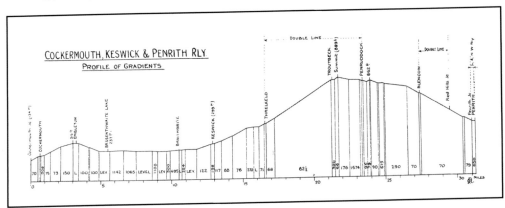

COCKERMOUTH, KESWICK & PENRITH RLY
PROFILE OF GRADIENTS

special interest in view of Thomas Bouch's notable viaducts on the Stainmore route and his ultimate – and fatal – concern with the bridging of the Tay and the design of a railway bridge (not built in the form he proposed) for the Firth of Forth.

During 1862-64, work seems to have proceeded without significant hitches or hold-ups under the direction of John Wood, Resident Engineer under Bouch, the latter being fully occupied elsewhere. Wood reported periodically to the Company's Board and Works Committee, which made its first trip by rail from Cockermouth to Keswick on 4 May 1864. They commented that the pitching (protective stonework) on the shore of Bassenthwaite Lake was of inferior material and workmanship, and must be renewed. On 1 June 1864 they travelled on an engine (would it be the property of the S&DR?) from Penrith station to Keswick station. On 13 July 1864 they traversed the full length of the line from Cockermouth to Penrith. Again, on 30 September 1864, they inspected the whole line, stating that the only obstacle to opening was 'the condition of the viaducts at Thornthwaite', delayed by non-delivery of timber. The subject of their concern would have been the screw-pile structures over low-lying lands on the Keswick side of Braithwaite station.

It is interesting that in March 1864 the C&WR agreed to lend a locomotive to the Keswick Company's contractors for 2 hours per day, for about a week, at £1 per day. Considerably later, on 29 November 1864, a C&WR engine was on loan to the Keswick Company, but the C&WR enginemen were being kept for excessive hours, and it was decided to withdraw the engine. Earlier, following the CKPR works committee's journey of 4 May, arrangements were made for the S&DR to hire to the CKPR and send to Mr Boulton a locomotive and 30 wagons – for use in ballasting. The loan dated from 25 May 1864 and was charged to the CKPR at £3 per day for the engine plus £1 monthly for each wagon.

Boultons probably had at least one locomotive of their own engaged from early days on the CKPR construction works: *Grant*,

an 0-4-0ST with 9in x 14in cylinders (clearly a small locomotive), built by Manning Wardle of Leeds, Works No 62 of 1862. It was despatched on 21 November 1862 to 'George Boulton & Son, Penrith'.

Again, on 19 February 1864, Isaac Watt Boulton, the locomotive dealer of Ashton-under-Lyne, sold to 'G. Boulton & Sons, contractors, Penrith' a four-coupled tank locomotive with outside cylinders (14in x 20in) and 4ft 9in diameter wheels (evidently much more powerful than *Grant*). Alfred Rosling Bennett, in his 'Chronicles of Boulton's Siding', reports this sale and states that the locomotive had been purchased not long before from the LNWR. Another reference in the same work *may* identify this locomotive with a type of outside-framed 0-4-2, having *inside* cylinders (14in x 20in) and 4ft 6in diameter wheels, built originally by Sharp Roberts & Company, of Manchester, as tender engines. There is also reason to believe that Boultons (of Penrith) secured the ownership, or use on hire, of a locomotive (from Gilkes Wilson & Company, locomotive builders, of Middlesbrough) during the course of the CKPR works.

Board of Trade inspections were made on 24 and 25 October 1864 by Capt F. H. Rich, RE. Opening of the line to minerals was effective from 4 November 1864, but the Captain declined to authorise passenger traffic on account of 11 listed shortcomings – notably the still incomplete pitching of the railway bank alongside Bassenthwaite Lake and the state of various abutments and parapet walls, as well as the lack of firm bearings for the wooden cross beams of some viaducts. Interestingly, the west Distant signal for Blencow, and its siting, was criticised, although Blencow was not a crossing place, nor understood to play a part in signalling in those early days. Thomas Bouch personally joined the Works Committee on a line inspection of 15 December and all were satisfied; so was Captain Rich on 22 December, and the confirmatory letter from the Board of Trade was dated 24 December, probably delivered at Keswick on Christmas Day.

Opening to passengers followed on 2

January 1865, seemingly without significant ceremony. The event was something of an anti-climax, as the opening should – by contract and anticipation – have been on 1 July 1864, and for long it was confidently expected that it would be achieved by the end of August 1864, with two days of special trains and a cold collation for guests. John Wood, as Thomas Bouch's Resident Engineer, earned the respect of the Company, which granted him a gratuity for 'extra services rendered during the construction of the line'. On 5 January 1865 he was appointed Company Engineer, the appointment to be effective on the ending of his commitment to Mr Bouch.

While the Railway Company went on to a passably successful career, its Board and its contractor enjoyed strained relations for many years. A dispute was proceeding in 1867-69, with a figure of £2,500 mentioned as likely to meet the contractor's claim. Ten years on, after awards by an arbitrator, then the Court of Appeal, the dispute continued during 1876-79 – nearly reaching the House of Lords – with the final cost to the Company, in 1879, approaching £5,000, presumably accompanied by handsome legal costs. As in many works of civil engineering, expenditure on additional requirements was central to the dispute.

* * *

Let us now embark upon a leisurely journey over the 40 miles of largely country railway from Workington to Penrith, via Cockermouth and Keswick, covering a time-scale of 125 years, from 1847 to 1972. This itinerary takes in the tiny Cockermouth & Workington Railway of 1847-66, with its subsequent career as part of a through route (1866-1966) leading to Cockermouth-Keswick (1865-1966) and Keswick-Penrith (1865-1972). For much of the time embraced, the first 6 miles (to Brigham) provided recurring glimpses of industry – it is smiling countryside today – while from just beyond bustling Cockermouth the scene is spectacular with fells, lake and mountains.

The second volume discusses permanent way, doubling of portions of the line, the many exciting bridges, its signalling and also the unique acetylene lighting – thus amplifying the descriptions in this itinerary. In summary, the stations and major junctions of the full route were:

Miles	**Station or junction**
0	Workington (Main)
¼	Derwent Junction
1¼	Workington Bridge Junction and station
3¼	Camerton
4½	Marron Junction
5¾	Broughton Cross
6½	Brigham
8¼	Cockermouth Junction
9	Cockermouth
11¾	Embleton
14¼	Bassenthwaite Lake
19¼	Braithwaite
21½	Keswick
25	Threlkeld
27¾	Highgate Platform
29¾	Troutbeck
32	Penruddock
36	Blencow
38	Redhills Junction
39¾	Penrith

This is the LMS version of September 1929 and is taken as broadly representing maximum development. The Up direction was from Workington to Penrith (namely, heading for Euston) and Down from Penrith to Workington. The terms Up and Down will be used without inverted commas, as in normal British and derived railway practice the world over. Our journey is in the Up direction, from west to east.

2. Workington to Brigham

Workington Main station

When, in 1866, the LNWR took over the Whitehaven Junction Railway's coastal route between Whitehaven, Workington and Maryport – as well as our Cockermouth & Workington Railway – the passenger station at Workington was an uninspired structure. It comprised two through passenger running lines, two platforms and poor buildings, but also a pair of goods lines to the west. Southward, blast furnaces only existed at Harrington and Cleator Moor. In Workington district, north of the Derwent, blast furnaces were found at Oldside Works and the newly established and progressive West Cumberland Works. There were no great flows of mineral traffic or products of the iron industry passing through the station. Soon, in 1872-73, the new works with blast furnaces at Whitehaven and also on Workington's southerly shore changed all this, and the railway's services were in constant demand by industry and its people.

Admittedly the Cleator Moor-Marron route began to offer a little relief, but only when the opening (from 1879) of the highly competitive Cleator & Workington Junction Railway brought into sharp focus the congestion on the coastal route did the LNWR take modernisation in hand.

A new layout at Workington Main was opened in November 1886, giving four roads through the station, with lengthy passenger platforms on the outer roads and further independent lines passing by on the west side; there was also a bay platform at the south end on the eastern side. The brick buildings of this new station for long looked dirty, drab and undistinguished, but cleaning and detailed improvements have revealed hitherto unsuspected colour and decoration, especially in the east front. This faces the small forecourt and access to the long Station Road.

Workington Main to Derwent Junction

Northwards, under the South Quay road bridge, the six tracks dating from the 1880s converged to form a double track across the Harbour Bridge, with the old harbour to westward, and the low-lying 'Cloffocks' were crossed. For many years the branch trailed in on the left from the Merchants Quay, so favoured in the 1850s for the loading of coals from the familiar chaldron wagons to seagoing vessels; after Lonsdale Dock was constructed, in 1865, the installations of the Quay declined in use.

The Derwent Viaduct follows closely. The cramped Lowther Iron Works, in production 1873-1911, but never a steel-producing works, was to the left. Now came the eastward divergence of the double-track route for Cockermouth, which we follow (albeit closed and abandoned in 1966), under the control of Derwent Junction signal box. This box also controlled the intriguing single-track lead of 1864, trailing off the Cockermouth line, crossing the coast route on the level and reaching Lonsdale Dock, which was remodelled and extended as the Prince of Wales Dock circa 1927. This trailing lead closed nominally wef' 21 February 1953. Oldside Iron Works (1841-1930, never steel-producing) was over to seaward of the coast line and West Cumberland Works (1862-1900, with steel production between 1870 and circa 1900) was on the landward side, having a trail-in at its south end into the Up Cockermouth line.

Taking the Cockermouth & Workington line eastward, it was crossed by a bridge

Left Workington station in the early 1880s, looking north. The layout shown is much as that taken over by the LNWR from the Whitehaven Junction Railway in 1866. The standard LNWR signal box in the middle distance was an addition. *Richard L. Pattinson/Cumbrian Railways Association (CRA)*

Right A similar view at Workington in April 1985, showing essentially the layout developed in the mid-1880s and the buildings of that period. *Harold D. Bowtell*

Below Workington station frontage in LNWR days. Children play while workmen enjoy a cigarette and a chat. *The Sankey Collection*

A southward view on the coastal main line, just north of Workington station. The Merchants Quay branch trailed into the main line for many years through its gate. In C&WR days (1847-66) most of the coal conveyed from pits a few miles inland were hauled in chaldron wagons to this branch, then exported by sea. *Richard L. Pattinson/CRA*

The scene at Derwent Junction, looking south. In the left background is the Derwent viaduct, with a footway beside it and the Merchants Quay branch slightly beyond the viaduct on the right. The main line to Workington station disappears into the mist. The Cockermouth (and Keswick and Penrith) route is just visible curving off sharply left (eastward). To the left of this field of view, the Keswick road was joined by the direct link from Lonsdale Dock and Lowther Iron Works, which crosses the main running lines close to the old Junction signal box. *Richard L. Pattinson collection/CRA*

carrying the double-track C&WJnR, dating from 1879-80; immediately southward the C&WJnR and the 'navvies bridge' footway also crossed the broad Derwent. Final closure of this section of the C&WJnR, between Harrington Junction, Workington Central and Calva Junction (north of the Cockermouth line) was recorded by British Railways as effective from Sunday 26 September 1965. The Cockermouth line then passed under the A596 and reached Workington Bridge.

Workington Bridge

Following pressure from residents of the higher, easterly part of the town, the station in basic form was first provided in 1847. Although the buildings were always modest, they enjoyed some rebuilding in 1867 and 1877. The station master occupied a house near the C&WJnR bridge. The station site was very cramped. Closure to passengers and goods was wef 1 January 1951. The Railway Company had a riverside pumphouse adjoining the station, with a lineside pipe to the large tank in Workington Main Yard; it supplied two locomotive water tanks and the needs of the locomotive shed.

Workington Bridge Junction signal box (on the right) controlled the C&WJnR double-track link of 16 March 1885 from Cloffocks Junction, with its own bridge over the Derwent and trail-in (also on the right) to the Cockermouth route. Very limited sidings existed for exchange of the vital coke traffic from County Durham to ironworks served by the C&WJnR, and the returning 'empties'. The traffic declined after about 25 years, rapidly after the First World War, and disappeared circa 1926. The line fell into disuse and its formal closure is obscure, but was probably in 1930. It was removed by 1933.

Derwent Tin Plate Works and Barepot (Beerpot) village

This site was 'tucked in' under the wooded bluff to the north of the Cockermouth line,

and a single-track branch diverged leftwards from the C&WR, actually trailing off the Down road across the Up line. It was one of the earliest sites exploited industrially in West Cumberland, and its lease from Sir James Lowther dated from 1762, with a blast furnace soon erected by Spedding Hicks & Co. A feeder canal from the Derwent, upstream, a mill reservoir and a tailrace to the river indicate water power, and their alignments necessitated three bridges to carry the C&WR (1847), these still being traceable today. Adam Heslop is understood to have designed a steam engine for the iron works in the 1790s. In 1819 the works came under common ownership with the Lowca Iron Works (which was at Parton). The proprietors, by then titled Tulk & Ley, are known for their building of main-line locomotives from 1840 onwards and, as Fletcher Jennings & Company, of industrial locomotives from 1858. The locomotives were built at Lowca Works.

From 1852 the Derwent Works belonged to Henderson & Davis/William Henderson, who manufactured iron bars in a puddling furnace near Workington harbour. The bars were conveyed to Barepot (Derwent), perhaps 2

Workington Bridge, the first station on the C&WR line from Workington, seen in LMS days. Workington Bridge signal box (closed around 1950) is just glimpsed above the LNWR timber station buildings. The station itself closed from 1 January 1951. *Richard L. Pattinson/CRA*

miles, where the rolling of tinplate commenced. It was during this period that the branch railway was laid. In February 1855 these proprietors advertised the following assets: a blast furnace, rolling mills, both water and steam power, and a railway branch to the works. By August 1856 Samuel Wagstaffe Smith/S. W. Smith & Company (alt: Derwent Tin Plate Company) was paying interest to the C&WR on the costs of making the siding. In that year the Railway was conveying coke and limestone from Workington to the site, and pig iron outwards (at April 1856). Later in the year the railway traffic comprised pig iron from Workington and export of tin in boxes from 'Beer Pot' to Merchants Quay. The C&WR's contemporary title for the traffic sidings was 'Seaton Iron Works'.

Smiths were soon (by January 1857) delaying the Railway Company's wagons and using them (contrary to injunctions) on the incline to their furnaces to deliver charges of ore. By December the Railway held five of the firm's own wagons as surety for unpaid debts. Three of Smiths' employees were prosecuted for walking on the C&WR main line, and fined. Soon after this incident, in 1857, it was recorded that 'another piece of wood has been found laid across the lines near Beerpot'!

Mr Spence was seemingly proprietor from 1858 to 1861, but with very intermittent operation of the blast furnace and despatch of tinplate to Workington. Surprisingly, 200 workers were said to be employed in 1860, but failure was reported in June 1861. After a brief period of production by Samuel Sandys Briggs,

of Workington, sale of the works was achieved in 1869 to William Ivander Griffiths, lately of Treforest, who came with a background in tinplate and a group of skilled men. A siding agreement of 12 January 1874 and opening for traffic on 11 June 1875 involved Messrs Griffiths and Walters and the LNWR. There were good years, then intermittent bad trade, and takeover of the works in 1885 by West Cumberland Hematite Iron & Steel Company Ltd – then closure in 1890, owing to their problems. LNWR records implied little rail traffic after 1881. Dismantlement, mainly in the 1890s but completed about 1909, has today left one building, used as a store for milk bottles, various ruined walls and water channels and a handsome new house of 1984-85 in the walled grounds of the one-time manager's 'Derwent House'. The imposing old entrance has gateposts, 'with knobs on'. The village includes a terrace of former tinplate workers' houses, and Workington's music festival traces its origins in the Eisteddfod brought by the Welshmen to the district.

The LNWR titled its signal box 'Derwent Tin Plate Works Sidings', but they and others down the years have referred to the works variously as Beer Pot, Beerpot, Barepotts and Barepot. The isolated LNWR house adjoins the site of 'Derwent Tin Plate Works Level Crossing'. A lane from Barepot village to the river side and Seaton Cornmill crossed the 'main line' here, right back to 1847, when it was known as Beer Pot Gate. The actual Works Sidings signal box was a block post until at least 1910, but by 1916 only had signals and indicators for protection of the

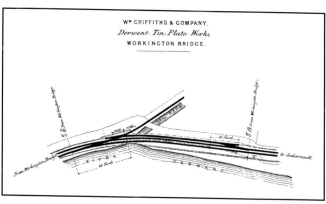

The branch into Derwent Tin Plate Works, Barepot, east of Workington Bridge: this is the 1874 plan, but the layout was virtually the same in the 1915 version, which includes a signal box in place of the tiny cabin (bottom right).

crossing, the siding connections being removed in 1916 and the box and signals (probably) in 1917. In latter days of the railway, during the 1960s, Mrs Briggs, at the house, was crossing keeper, while her husband Henry held a railway post in Workington.

Seaton Mill

Travelling eastward from Barepot, the mill race was on the left of the line, and was shortly crossed, with the broad and swift-flowing Derwent close at hand on the right. The water-driven Seaton Corn Mill eventually became an adjunct of the adjoining farm – all forming an attractive group of buildings between the railway and the river.

Immediately eastward again was Seaton Mill Level Crossing, styled Seaton Gate in 1847. Its stone-built house, on the Up side, is not of obvious LNWR origin and is still a residence. No fewer than four bridges followed in close succession: No 37 over the mill race, No 36 (Byefalls) over the subsidiary channel, and Nos 34 and 33 (Salmon Hall Nos 2 and 1) over the main channels of the Derwent. Salmon Hall and the associated buildings form another pleasant group in open lands to the left of the railway route.

William Pit Sidings

Within the wide arm of the Derwent, between Salmon Hall No 1 and Stainburn bridges, a considerable layout developed on the Down (right) side, with a signal box on the Up side and a private single-track mineral railway climbing from the sidings steeply south-

eastward to William Pit Colliery, more than a mile distant, near Great Clifton village. This colliery superseded the various coal pits of the Fletcher family, which had provided the C&WR of 1847-66 with its main reason for construction and its principal traffic. Already in 1865 I. & W. Fletcher & Company were sinking their new William Pit colliery at Clifton and suggested to the C&WR that they would need to connect by private tramway to the railway, primarily for shipments via Workington Harbour. They saw alternatives of connecting at Lowther Pit Siding, at Camerton station, or between Stainburn and Salmon Hall bridges. In September-October 1865 the C&WR agreed in principle to install two pairs of points and crossings to connect with the sidings to be laid by Fletchers and to put a small arch in the wall of the overbridge connecting portions of the Stainburn Estate. The over-line occupation bridge in later times had a 29-foot span over the Colliery Company's sidings and 17 feet over the LNWR.

William Pit of Clifton Collieries was leased from 1873 by the West Cumberland Hematite Iron & Steel Company Ltd, of Workington, but taken over by Allerdale Coal Company on its formation in 1887 and worked by that company and the National Coal Board in succession. The junction signal box in its final form dated back to circa 1881 and the Colliery locomotives are traceable back to 1890; there were three for most of the 20th century, until closure in 1959, and dismantling by Cohens in 1961. The signal box remained open as a

Seaton Mill level crossing and crossing house are depicted, looking east, with the lever frame at the foot of the right-hand signal. Over-line bridge No 31, at William Pit Sidings, can be discerned in the distance. *Richard L. Pattinson/CRA*

Above A westbound passenger train, hauled by a 'Cauliflower' 0-6-0, is seen crossing the Salmon Hall bridges over the River Derwent. This is believed to be the No 1 bridge, which had three spans aggregating 125 feet in length. *Richard L. Pattinson/CRA*

Below William Pit Sidings (1874 plan) depicted during the period after the West Cumberland Company had taken over from the Fletcher family company.

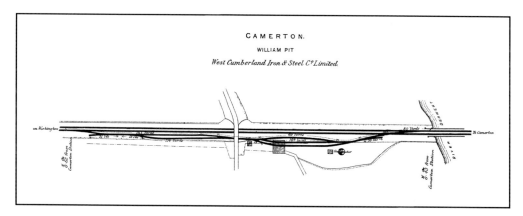

block post until January 1965. In 1983-84 the lands at 'William Pit Sidings' (site of) were in part reclaimed for farming and the overbridge abutments became a heap of stones. The steep route by which the privately owned colliery locomotives laboured with their 'empties' can still be followed today.

Camerton station

Eastward of Stainburn Bridge the railway soon reached the attractive over-line bridge that still carries the lane to the isolated church of St Peter and its graveyard. A byway formerly crossed the line on the level, before Camerton station, where the two station houses (dating probably from 1882) on the Down platform have been combined, by building on the yard that separated them, and also extended as a present-day residence.

The station was an original C&WR facility. It acquired a timber booking office and waiting room circa 1879, before the houses were added. It closed to passengers and freight wef 3 March 1952, about a year after the demise of Workington Bridge station. This was the period (circa 1946-1956) when the LMS and BR (LMR) eliminated little-used stations one by one, but without accompanying the closures with any constructive overall plan for compensatory

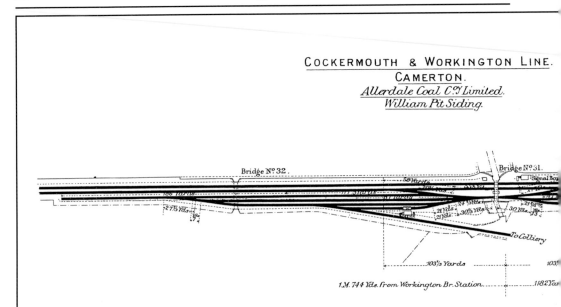

COCKERMOUTH & WORKINGTON LINE.
CAMERTON.
Allerdale Coal C.º Limited.
William Pit Siding.

Above The 1916 version of William Pit Sidings shows their development and the private branch railway heading off to the Allerdale Company's colliery on the hill south-eastward.

Below William Pit Sidings signal box (c1881-1965) is framed by the over-line accommodation bridge as a westbound goods passes. The 'Cauliflower' is carrying a 12D shedplate (Workington, post-1935). A Kilmarnock-built (Andrew Barclay) saddle-tank locomotive owned by the Allerdale Coal Company is working beneath the right-hand span. *Richard L. Pattinson/CRA*

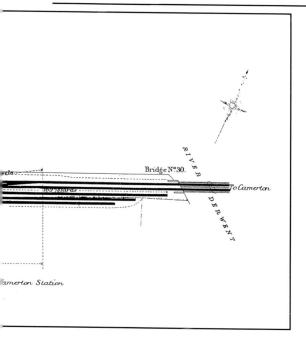

the Railway-owned footbridge, now rebuilt by the County Council.

Camerton Colliery and Brickworks

Between the station and Camerton Bridge over the River Derwent, the colliery site was on the Up side of the line. The C&WR opened on 27 April 1847 and on Wednesday 2 June 1847 the first train of coals was run over the new line. It was despatched from the Greengill Colliery, Camerton, of William Thornburn, who resided at Papcastle, for shipment at Workington. The Railway's locomotive *Cocker* hauled 21 loaded wagons. Ten years later Mr Thornburn was still consigning coals from here for shipment, but in small quantities. William Thornburn Junior was a member of the C&WR board from 1856 to 1863. In 1859 bricks were forthcoming from Camerton (Mr Cook) for conveyance to both Cockermouth and Workington. The coal came out of drift mines or 'levels' in the hillside behind the colliery buildings and, by the later 19th century, from Wood Drift just to the north, tubways being employed from the drifts to the colliery screens from as early as 1864. Camerton Colliery & Brickworks Company were the proprietors by the 1870s.

Later came Camerton Brick & Coal Company (J. Mulcaster), subsequently amended to the Camerton Colliery Company. By April 1917 it was Camerton Coal, Fireclay & Ganister Company (Messrs Mutch), for whom the LNWR put the sidings in order. Then, from May 1919, the Camerton Coal &

acceleration and improvement of services between busier centres.

Although essentially Camerton closed wef 3 March 1952 as stated, there was an unadvertsied 'Fridays only' call by the westbound 9.52am from Carlisle (10.20 from Penrith), a diesel multiple unit, several years later.

A devious lane came down from Camerton village, located on higher ground to the north, and a mile-long and even more hilly footpath connected with Great Clifton village on the ridge southward, crossing the Derwent river by

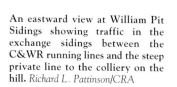

An eastward view at William Pit Sidings showing traffic in the exchange sidings between the C&WR running lines and the steep private line to the colliery on the hill. *Richard L. Pattinson/CRA*

Firebrick Co Ltd were in possession. The next owners, from 1935, were Camerton Firebrick & Coal Co Ltd (controlled by J. & J. Dyson Ltd, fireclay manufacturers, of Hunnington, Sheffield), with a siding agreement that was adjusted on 26 February 1938. Wilkinsons' Wagon Works used part of the site and produced rail movements. T. McKay & Sons (Fireclay & Concrete Products Ltd) of St Bees took over the works and sidings in January 1939, with a siding agreement of 15 March 1940.

However, the Admiralty had established a depot at Broughton Moor, absorbing the Allerdale Coal Company's Buckhill Colliery, closed in 1939, and part of the former C&WJnR 'Northern Extension line' (which had extended in its time between Calva Junction-Seaton-Buckhill Colliery-Great Broughton-Linefoot). This development led to the Admiralty establishing a depot for

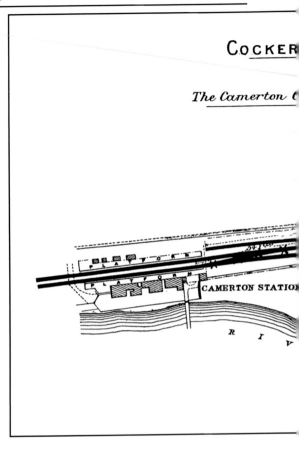

COCKER

The Camerton (

CAMERTON STATION

Right East of Camerton station, the lead into the Camerton colliery and brickworks is seen, probably during the 1930s. *Richard L. Pattinson/CRA*

Below Camerton station and the C&WR's connection to the Camerton Coal & Firebrick Company, as depicted by an LNWR plan of December 1917. In earlier days the station had its own signal box. *Author's collection*

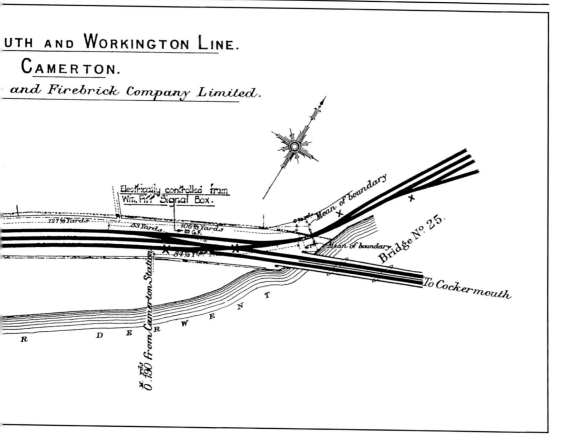

UTH AND **WORKINGTON LINE.**

CAMERTON.

and Firebrick Company Limited.

ammunition in Camerton clay mine. At their instance, the Camerton sidings (C&WR line) were extended; the work was carried out between October 1941 and February 1942 and December 1942 and May 1943, with a fresh siding agreement negotiated between February and September 1947. In (or by) 1950 Sebrix Ltd, of Newcastle-upon-Tyne, took over the sidings from the Admiralty, the agreement with BR being dated 30 September 1953, with amendments in 1957. They provided high-quality firebricks, but the brickworks premises were demolished in 1956-57.

Wilkinsons may well have reappeared in the post-war years, breaking up wagons here. The signal box, for many years open 'as required', was replaced by a ground frame in 1935.

The site of the railway lead-in to Camerton's colliery and brickworks activities is still clear to see and in 1984 one building still stood, although landscaping was in hand. The lead was reached by setting back off the Up line and drawing forward to the branch or, earlier again, by setting back across the road from the Down main line. Just west of this point there is a hint of a probable one-time tramway, maybe from early drift mines, running southward to the river and crossing in its course the alignment used by the railway.

Ribton Hall Sidings

Beyond Camerton Bridge over the Derwent and the ensuing Ribton Bridge of six spans, there were short-lived sidings on the Up side of the running lines. Under the title 'Ribton Hall Sidings', and an agreement of 1 October 1873 between I. & W. Fletcher (also Edward Waugh) and the LNWR, two connections were put in, 13 chains apart. These were completed and opened to traffic in April

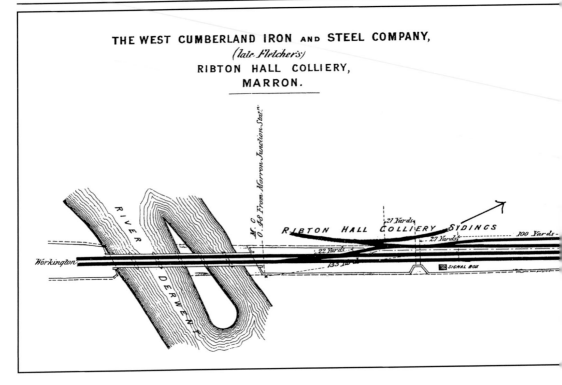

THE WEST CUMBERLAND IRON AND STEEL COMPANY,
(late Fletcher's)
RIBTON HALL COLLIERY,
MARRON.

1874, the West Cumberland Hematite Iron & Steel Company having meanwhile taken over; an agreement with the LNWR dated 27 September 1876 ratified the change. The property reverted to Messrs Fletcher and Waugh in March 1887, but the sidings were closed by then, or soon after, and were lifted in November 1888. It is particularly interesting that, in the period 1874-1878, the Iron Company ran its engine between Lowther Pit (mentioned later) and Ribton Sidings, thus traversing the LNWR double track over Ribton High Bridge in their trips to and fro. Until 1878 a signalman was maintained at Ribton, in charge of the points.

A gradually descending footpath from the vicinity of Buckhill Colliery (northward of the C&WR line) to the route may have followed the course of a tramroad to the river – possibly of earlier date than the 1873 project. The third crossing of the Derwent between Camerton and Marron was by Ribton High Bridge. This brought the line to sites of earlier industry, and to the railway junctions at Marron.

Ribton Hall Sidings (located between two bridges over the Derwent) only existed from 1874 to 1888; this plan is of 1874. By the time of the Ordnance Survey in 1898, the private branch line (arrowed) was a footpath.

Early coal pits: Lowther, Harrygill, Linefitts and others

The Fletcher family were leading promoters of the C&WR – they provided its successive Chairmen and its staple traffic in coals to Workington. The Railway Company had to steer a careful course between extracting maximum revenue from Isaac & William Fletcher & Company, yet also obliging them in every way. It was a difficult balance to achieve, for lesser coal-owner clients, represented by Directors and shareholders, were ever ready to criticise if more favourable terms were accorded to the Fletchers.

The Fletchers developed Clifton Old Pit (as it became known) from 1827, and Crossbarrow (alt: Crossbarron) followed – both in the relatively elevated country traversed by the Workington-Cockermouth Road. Lowther Colliery (from 1852) was in

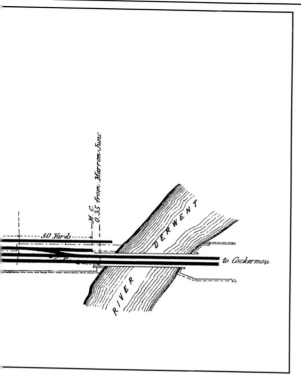

the C&WR; indeed, even in 1847 a switchman was required for 'Fletcher's Siding'. Clifton and Crossbarrow were sending coals by 'the Marron branch', which would be this 'Siding', but the Fletchers proposed building a tramway to link them with Lowther Pit Sidings or Harrygill Siding. On 20 October 1856 they pressed their demand for seven years of preferential terms by writing to the C&WR Board, emphasising that a private tramway from the pits to Workington harbour would be more direct and economical to operate than the existing arrangement. Lord Lonsdale was said to own virtually all the necessary land and it was claimed that he had given his consent. The Railway's Board speedily accorded them a meeting and agreed special terms.

Strenuous objections from shareholders followed, but broadly the terms were amicably agreed by the general meeting of 31 January 1857. The complete tramway to the C&WR does not seem to have been built, but a link was constructed from Westray Pit, with a concluding steep descent to Lowther Colliery. A decade or so later the old pits in the hinterland were replaced by the Fletchers' new William Pit, of which the later ownership has been discussed. This brought early beehive ovens to Lowther Colliery, used to provide

the meadow south-east of the C&WR's Ribton High Bridge and was skirted by the railway. Westray Pit was up the hill behind, towards the main road and Crossbarrow. Harrygill Pit was close to the railway, between Lowther Colliery and Marron Junctions. By 1856 Lowther and Harry Gill had sidings on

The lead-in from Lowther Pit, in its early form, as recorded on the LNWR's plan of 1874.

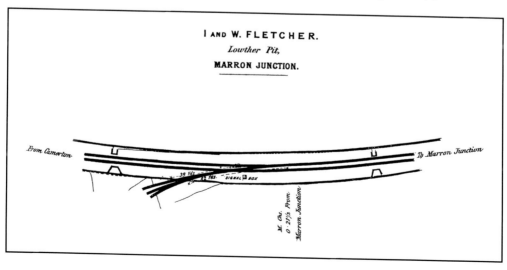

TRUSTEES OF THE LATE W. HARRIS.

Linefitz Colliery.

MARRON JUNCTION.

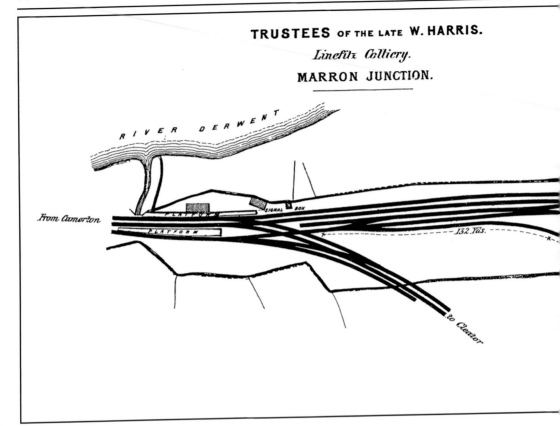

COCKERMOUTH AND WORKINGTON LINE.
MARRON JUNCTION.

Allerdale Coal Cº
Lowther Pit Siding.

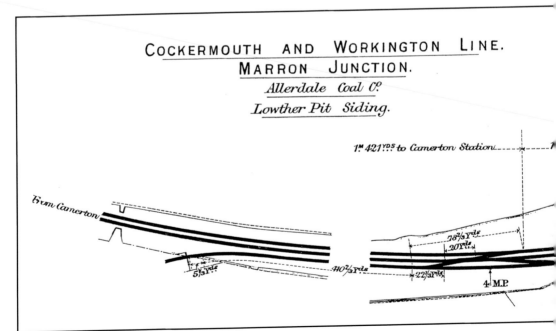

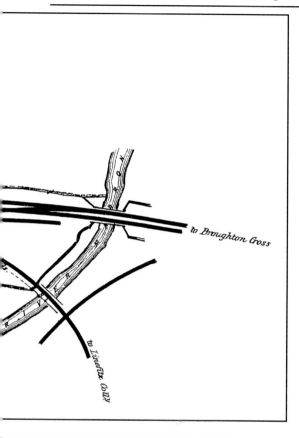

coke for the lessees' blast furnaces at Workington – more traffic for the C&WR's successors.

The Allerdale Coal Company took over at Lowther in 1887, from West Cumberland Hematite Iron & Steel Company, along with the modern William Pit; there was a Fletcher interest in Allerdale, but in later years Directors from South Yorkshire were prominent. Lowther Colliery was closed, and by January 1893 only brickworks traffic remained. Lowther Colliery Siding, with its link to the Joint Line under control of Marron Junction signal box, survived, almost moribund (the subject of a limited rental in the period 1915-21), but was disused as a stub of line in 1923. Its site and that of the tramway from Westray are still clear on the ground.

Linefitts Colliery was the only mine in the vicinity not owned by the Fletchers and was in the Harris family, a recurring name on the C&WR Board. In 1854 its access was by a short south-east curve off the C&WR's Marron loop line; the east curve from the 'Joint Line' to the C&WR was built across it 'on the level' in 1866. Joseph Harris, of Greysouthen, constructed the private branch from the pit to its timber bridge over the Marron (inclusive) in 1847, and the C&WR connected it to their original Siding, namely the Railway's 'Marron Branch'.

The Greysouthen (pronounced 'Greysoon') Colliery of Joseph Harris & Company was in the country south-eastward of Marron Junctions and was never fully rail-connected – but by 1857 it was consigning shipment coals in small quantities, via the C&WR, to Workington, and in 1859 Captain John Harris (died 1863) of this Company, who was also a Director of the C&WR, was preparing to send coals from Marron Sidings to

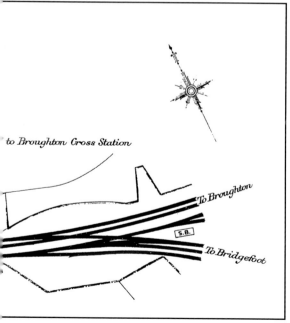

By 1916, Lowther Pit had long closed and its brickworks was moribund. The large signal box of 1902-60 is seen in the angle of the west junction, at Marron.

Maryport. The Harris Company is on record in 1865 as planning to employ its own private-owner wagons over the C&WR.

By February 1870 the wooden bridge had become unsafe for the passage of Railway Company engines, so men from the pits pushed the wagons across by hand, but by this date the pit was virtually worked out. The bridge and the private line beyond (east) were removed before 1887, when the siding rent ceased to be paid.

Marron Junctions

The railway layout here was essentially triangular, with West and East Junctions on the C&WR line and a South Junction on the route to Cleator Moor – this was the WC&ER, which became the FR & LNWR 'Joint Line'. Favoured opening dates at Marron are 15 January 1866 (minerals) and 2 April 1866 (passengers), seemingly on both east and west curves. The first Ordnance Survey, of 1864, shows a complete layout, with the C&WR main line then single, and a passenger platform on its north side, just on the Workington side of the West Junction. There was double track on the west curve and single on the east curve, a single track from the South Junction to Bridgefoot and double track at Bridgefoot station. A loop line for mineral traffic paralleled the C&WR from near the Lowther Colliery connection, past the Harrygill connection and as far east as the Linefitts Colliery branch. The route of that early branch, described above, is even today identifiable at the site of its timber bridge over the Marron river and its crossing of the east curve a little to the north of, and behind, Marron Junction locomotive shed.

A single pointsman had charge of Lowther Pit Siding, Harrygill Siding and Marron Siding in the C&WR's early days, but the junctions of 1866 called for pointsmen in their respective cabins, and from about 1871 LNWR signal boxes were in use at the three corners of the triangle. By this time the C&WR route (LNWR) was double track and a southerly island platform figured by 1874, possibly installed when the line was doubled. The passenger station, such as it was, had been constructed at the joint expense of the C&WR and WC&ER in its initial form and was intended solely for changing trains. It officially closed to passengers wef 1 July 1897. Direct working of the odd cattle or passenger train between the 'Joint Line' and Cockermouth ceased with the taking out of the East Junction in (it is believed) 1902. A new signal box was built at that time near West Junction.

Much later, on 7 November 1960, it in turn was replaced by a ground frame of two levers. The short portion of the 'Joint Line' between Bridgefoot and Marron Junction (meaning the new west junction) was still double in 1924, although converted later to single track. From Rowrah to Marron Junction normal traffic ceased in November 1953, with an official closure date of wef 3 May 1954. The 'West Cumberland Rail Tour', a special passenger train for the Stephenson Locomotive Society and the Manchester

The western approach to Marron Junction. The independent line from the Lowther Colliery site is in the foreground, to the right of the double running lines – note the ground signals mounted on the cutting sides. The main-line signal is 'off' for the Cockermouth route; the right-hand signal arm controls the divergence (right of the box) to the 'Joint Line' for Rowrah and Cleator Moor. *Richard L. Pattinson/CRA*

Locomotive Society, was privileged to run through, northbound, on 5 September 1954. After years of disuse, the final abandonment between Rowrah and Marron Junction was wef 7 November 1960, followed eventually by lifting.

The Marron river was crossed just west of the one-time Marron East Junction; the bridge survives and the layouts here are interesting to reconstruct on the ground today.

Melgramfitz Pit

A siding connection was made in the latter half of 1860, about half-way between Marron East Junction (to be) and Broughton Cross station, in order to serve this new colliery, then being sunk by the Fletcher family. Two tracks passed through the screens and connected at the west and east ends to the running line. Coals were first despatched in November 1863 and production continued through the 1870s, the West Cumberland Hematite Iron & Steel Company being proprietors from 1873. The colliery became exhausted in 1880 and the rail connections were taken out in July-October 1883. The site is lost today in the A66 road of the 1970s.

Broughton Cross station

This was an original station on the C&WR, with a bend in the Derwent sweeping close by to its north. In 1864 it had one siding on the single line, but the ensuing double-track layout provided no sidings or goods facilities. The substantial stone buildings were on the Down platform, adjoining the (old) main road and village, in which some houses were built by the Fletchers for workers at Melgramfitz Colliery of 1860. The station was never a block post and it closed wef 2 March 1942, a wartime economy. The buildings survive today as a house, while the A66 road occupies, broadly, the railway alignment.

The village of Greysouthen is about a mile south of Broughton Cross station, while Tarn Bank is to the east of the road to the village. It figured in the 1850s as residence of both Isaac and William Fletcher, the coal-owners; also of John Wilson Fletcher, Chairman of the C&WR for most of the years 1845-1857. Isaac Fletcher, of Tarn Bank, was son of J. W.

Fletcher, and became Chairman of the CKPR from 1867; he was also MP for Cockermouth from 1868 to 1879.

Hotchberry limestone quarry

The Hotchberry limestone quarry was located to the east side of the Brigham-Eaglesfield road, about 1¼ miles from Broughton Cross station and about 1 mile south of the village of Brigham. Jno Todhunter, the proprietor at that time, signed a siding agreement with the LNWR on 8 June 1883. The 'Hotchberry Limestone Siding' was to be at Broughton Cross, presumably on the Down side of the double track, and Mr Todhunter planned to build a tramway from the siding to his quarries. In the event neither tramway nor siding were built, and the scheme was abandoned on 19 June 1885.

The quarry was the only one in the vicinity to remain in operation in 1923, and the output went by road to the railway at Brigham, like that of Ellerbeck limestone quarry – which employed two generations of steam lorries for haulage. The Hotchberry quarry used its own horses and carts for the trip to Brigham Limestone Siding, so it is recalled.

Brigham limestone sidings

From west of Broughton Cross station to Brigham station, and beyond, the route of the line today is occupied by the A66 road. Approaching Brigham station from the west, sidings were laid on the Down side at MP2 (from Cockermouth old station) to handle output from Brigham limestone quarry and kilns. Captain Harris, a member of the C&WR Board, was principal of the limeworks, from which consignments were being made to Whitehaven in 1856, using by arrangement wagons belonging to the Whitehaven Junction Railway. Traffic expanded and in 1860 agreement was given for the Captain to construct a standard gauge tramroad from the firm's kilns to the sidings. The resulting branch and layout was well depicted in the Ordnance Survey of 1863-64, also being shown by the LNWR on its diagrams of 1874 and 1915, by which latter date the owners were the Allerdale Coal Company. The tramroad passed diagonally

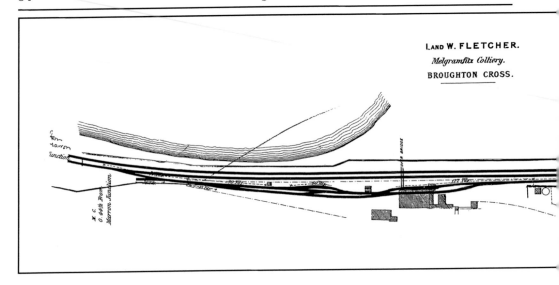

LAND W. FLETCHER.
Melgramfitz Colliery.
BROUGHTON CROSS.

Above Melgramfitz Colliery screens and loading siding were in the next section east of Marron. This plan shows the layout in 1874.

Below Broughton Cross station had neither sidings nor signalling, but the Up Distant signal for Brigham is prominent in this eastward view. *Richard L. Pattinson/CRA*

BROUGHTON CROSS

under the old main road near the Limekiln Inn. Workings and layout expanded, but were abandoned by the early 1920s, leaving an impressive hole at the quarry site.

The West Cumberland Hematite Iron & Steel Co Ltd, which produced pig iron from 1862 and steel from 1872, developed its own limestone quarry at Brigham by 1872. This had an internal narrow gauge line and a short standard gauge branch to the same sidings. Its lines were clearly delineated in 1898, but they disappeared early in the 20th century; indeed, the LNWR recorded lifting its own connection to these (one-time WCHIS Co

Ltd) private sidings in March 1910. From 1882, by activating a section of the Brigham Station Agreement of 1 January 1878, Maryport & Carlisle Railway locomotives started working to and from the limestone sidings, sharing traffic with the LNWR.

Brigham station
The level crossing and road to Brigham village curtailed the limestone sidings at their east end. In 1847 the crossing was known as Brigham Gate. The station was immediately to its east, with the original single platform on the south side of the line and good stone

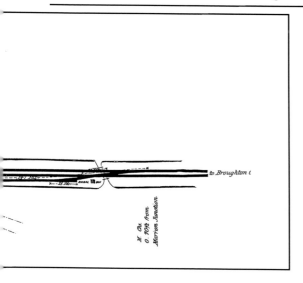

to Broughton (

M. Or.
0. 70M from
Marron Junction

buildings erected in 1863. Doubling of the track by the LNWR during 1868 and the opening in the previous year (wef 1 June 1867) of the M&CR line from Bullgill (and thus from Carlisle, by way of its main line) prompted the construction of an Up platform, with a back platform face for M&CR use. A turntable at the extremity of this M&CR road (in early days) and an independent run-round loop facilitated reversal of the Carlisle-Brigham-Cockermouth trains.

From the outset the M&CR exercised running powers to Cockermouth, although their running powers to Marron do not seem to have been used on any regular basis. The LNWR shuttled over the M&CR's massive

Derwent bridge to reach Broughton Craggs Quarry, at Papcastle. Papcastle Limestone Siding derived from an LNWR agreement (with the Allerdale Coal Company) of 14 December 1889. A further agreement, of 15 July 1910 (with Walker Brothers) provided for extension into their freestone quarry at Papcastle.

From 29 April 1935 the M&CR line was closed by the LMS, although some 20 years later the station signs on the M&CR route still declared 'Bullgill, change for Cockermouth'. From 16 May 1960 the Brigham to Cockermouth Junction section reverted to single track, with the Down road being in general the one abandoned. Total closure of Brigham passenger station, with the Derwent Junction-Cockermouth route, was wef 18 April 1966. The goods yard, connected to the M&CR branch until its demise, was closed wef 1 June 1964.

Away back in 1856 establishment of coal cells at Brigham, on the S&DR/NER model for bottom-door wagons, was agreed following a request by the Fletchers, as coal-owners. In

Brigham station, looking east over the level crossing, showing the sturdy stone buildings of 1863 adjacent to the Down platform and the LMS-design (Midland-derived) signal box of 1933. The loading dock for limestone is located in the foreground – the quarry branch once climbed away to the right – and 'Old Vicarage' farm (see text) is apparent, the church being out of sight on the right. The scene is from April 1968, two years after total closure of the Keswick-Workington section. *Harold D. Bowtell*

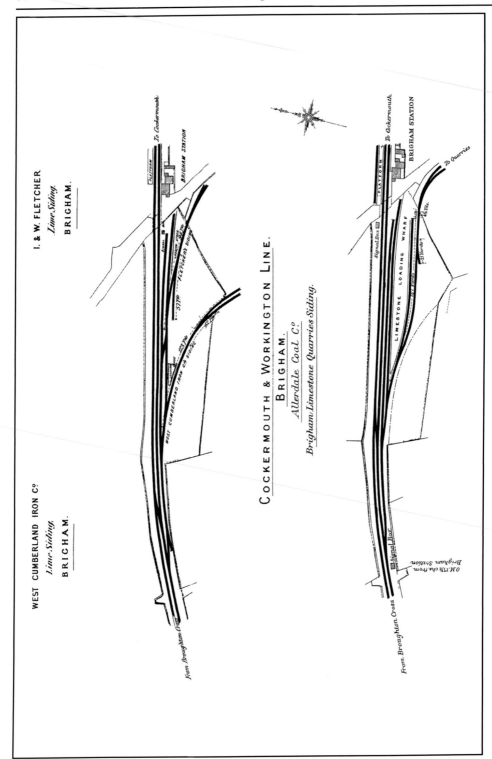

LNWR plans of May 1874 (above) and 1915 showing the developing private siding arrangements at Brigham station. *Author's collection*

This delightful scene depicts the Up platform at Brigham in pre-Grouping days. The train has come via Bullgill, maybe from Carlisle. The engine has run round and is seen signalled to emerge on to the LNWR and head for Cockermouth. The attractive LNWR bracket signal provides for running from Workington to the MCR (left) or Cockermouth (ahead). The locomotive may be MCR No R1 (No 19 until 1884), a 2-4-0 with 6-foot driving wheels built in 1867 at Maryport. *J. D. Hinde collection*

1858 the depot was a traffic siding where coal and coke could be handled. Through into BR days several merchants received and distributed coal from here.

Brigham church and vicarage

St Bridget's church is sited beside the road from Broughton High Bridge (over the Derwent) to Brigham village. The Rector from 1833 to 1875 was the Reverend John Wordsworth MA, eldest son of the poet William Wordsworth. About the time of his appointment John and his father chose a delectable site for his vicarage, with an extensive garden northward of the house and ending only on the river bank. Trouble followed, therefore, when the C&WR's 'plans and sections', accompanying its Bill in 1844, showed a railway route running roughly midway between the vicarage and the river, bisecting the garden. When the Act of 21 July 1845 received the Royal Assent, it included a 29th clause providing for the construction of a new vicarage at the Company's cost. In December 1845 the Reverend Mr Wordsworth and architect Charles Eaglesfield were consulted, a site was selected south-eastward of the church, and the Railway placed the building contract. This allowed £590 for taking down and rebuilding the vicarage, but in fact a new building was put up and handed over in June 1847. It is interesting to note that the Wordsworths invested in the

C&WR, with £500 of mortgage bonds allocated to William in December 1846 and £200 to John in the next month; interest was payable at 4½% per annum.

The location is nowadays less delectable, as the railway has been exchanged for a busy trunk road. The 'Old Vicarage', on rising ground south of the LNWR/M&CR junction, ante-dated the vicarage house of circa 1833 and was already Vicarage Farm in 1847. It remained occupied in 1985, still as a farm.

The steam lorry *Vino* outside its shed in Higher Brigham, with Harry Wire and Tommy Dunn in attendance, circa 1910. The lorry carried coal from Brigham station yard to Ellerbeck limestone quarry, and stone from the quarry to the loading dock. *J. D. Hinde collection*

3. Cockermouth

Cockermouth, 1847-1865

The Cockermouth & Workington Railway opened its terminal station on 27 April 1847, initially as a temporary structure. Its approach by rail was restricted by an awkward bend in the river on the northern side of the site, and the main road and the Senhouse family estate in the south. The road was slightly diverted to accommodate the railway, but a cramped site resulted, well short of the built-up area of the town. Accommodation at the east end of the site included a goods warehouse, with two tracks and wagon turntables, while coal merchants' cells were provided by the main road. A small covered passenger station was squeezed between shed and cells and a locomotive turntable was located at the north-western extremity of the site. Adjoining was a locomotive shed with two tracks and ancillary buildings and two more roads to its north. Here were based the C&WR's locomotives – three initially and five eventually – together with the Company's workshops.

The Cockermouth, Keswick & Penrith Railway, constructed 1862-64, made a physical junction with the C&WR significantly west of the terminal station, in order to ease the curve and rising gradient on their chosen route. One notes that the C&WR line approached Cockermouth as single track until early in 1868, when it was doubled, but the CKPR route climbed away from the junction on single track – never doubled – and skirted the southern border of the town, past the gasworks, to reach Cockermouth (upper) station. This was designed from the start for through running of passenger trains between Workington, Keswick and Penrith. Commercial mineral traffic started nominally on 4 November 1864, passenger traffic on 2 January 1865.

Cockermouth stations, 1865-1876

Representatives of the C&WR and CKPR met at Workington on 28 January 1864, with W. N. Hodgson, a Director of the LNWR and also by then of the CKPR, present. It was decided that passenger traffic would be concentrated on the new (upper) station at Cockermouth, where the M&CR services would also be handled. C&WR and CKPR mineral and merchandise traffic would use the C&WR (lower) site. The coal depot here was to remain unchanged; with some extension, it lasted until 1964, and was in use in the 1980s, although not rail served. The C&WR

Below Cockermouth goods station layout.

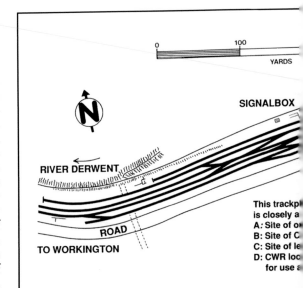

passenger station became a 'temporary' goods station for both Companies, their existing goods building being taken down.

The LNWR took over the Whitehaven Junction Railway and the C&WR in mid-1866. On 1 August 1866 Richard Moon,

Right An eastward vista from Cockermouth Junction. The original route of 1847 (double line) leads to the (lower) goods station, taking in the C&WR's cramped passenger and goods site. The CKPR route (opened 1864-65) climbs steeply on its right-hand curve, heading for the (upper) passenger station. The extremity of 'the Stockton siding' is on the right; it was used for holding westbound coke trains from S&DR territory before 'tripping' of the traffic to West Cumberland's ironworks. *Richard L. Pattinson/CRA*

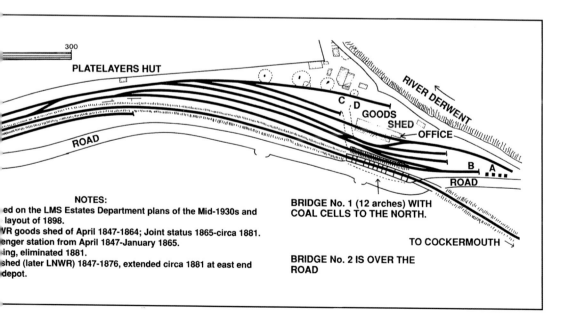

NOTES:
...ed on the LMS Estates Department plans of the Mid-1930s and
 layout of 1898.
...VR goods shed of April 1847-1864; Joint status 1865-circa 1881.
...enger station from April 1847-January 1865.
...ing, eliminated 1881.
...shed (later LNWR) 1847-1876, extended circa 1881 at east end
...depot.

BRIDGE No. 1 (12 arches) WITH
COAL CELLS TO THE NORTH.

TO COCKERMOUTH

BRIDGE No. 2 IS OVER THE
ROAD

Chairman of the LNWR, travelled via Penrith and the CKPR line, then in its second year of passenger operation (but not, be it noted, ownership) by the LNWR. He was bound for Whitehaven, doubtless to view critically his new domains, their facilities and staffs. With Mr Moon present, a meeting was held in the Boardroom at Cockermouth upper station. The management of this station was to be shared by Henry Cattle, Secretary and Manager of the CKPR, and John Mayson (who restyled himself John Myson about this time). Mr Mayson had been the last Secretary and General Manager of the C&WR and became District Manager of the LNWR's West Cumberland lines and secretary of the Cockermouth joint station committee – until his resignation from the service around August 1869. No LNWR Director was appointed to the joint station committee at this time, in 1866, but by 1881 the LNWR was represented by Richard Moon and William Cawkwell, respectively Chairman and General Manager, with Miles McInnes (LNWR Director, of Carlisle) replacing Richard Moon in 1883. The CKPR also included a Director among its two members.

From 1 November 1867 the M&CR was given full use of the new joint station at Cockermouth, including 'for sidings and carriage sheds'; they were to work traffic from and to their system. In the same year it was decided to construct a cattle loading dock adjoining the upper passenger station, to supersede the cramped arrangements at the lower site. This early provision for expansion

was justified in after years. Less foresight was shown concerning the goods station, still in the cramped, former passenger building at the lower site.

In January 1876 the dilapidated condition of the office was blamed by Mr Bewsher, the goods agent, for the poor health of the clerks and himself, and for the accounts falling into arrears. He was cautioned and assistance was proposed, but by 9 February 1876 he had absconded, leaving a deficiency in his accounts. He was dismissed in absentia and Mr Patrickson, Chief Goods Clerk at Penrith, was appointed in his stead, with a salary of £100pa.

Cockermouth locomotive sheds

The LNWR provided motive power for the CKPR passenger and goods trains from the opening of that line in 1865, and from 1867 it was doing the same job for its own newly acquired C&WR and Workington Junction lines. A minute of January 1864 (meeting at Cockermouth) had recorded that sufficient accommodation would be provided for engines working the traffic of the Keswick Company, either 'in connection with the present engine shed or at such other site as may hereafter be agreed upon...' The 'present shed' was at Cockermouth. It was soon supplemented by a shed at Penrith and, from 1876, by a large locomotive shed at Workington.

The NER locomotives that came through from Kirkby Stephen with mineral traffic for West Cumberland did not proceed beyond the

This was the C&WR's two-road locomotive shed of circa 1847, seen from the west in September 1966. It was extended by 25 feet in 1858 (represented by the fourth and fifth arches in the side wall) and, after probably a ten-year span housing LNWR locomotives, it was further extended east to form a new goods shed. *Harold D. Bowtell*

lower yard at Cockermouth. They were serviced by their crews and, after turning, worked back east. Thus they did not initially require a locomotive shed at Cockermouth. However, there was an early undertaking, or at least implication, that the former C&WR shed would be available to the NER. It was some ten years later, in December 1875, when J. E. McNay, Secretary of the NER's Darlington Section (doubtless based on the old S&DR) approached Peter Thompson, by then Secretary and General Manager of the CKPR, with a proposition. The NER planned to work its traffic between Kirkby Stephen and Clifton under block signalling regulations, and when this took effect they would need to station two locomotives at Cockermouth (sic). Mr McNay presumed – maybe tongue-in-cheek – that there would be no difficulty, as the CKPR 'already have the accommodation for two of our engines'. After inconclusive exchanges, the issue lay dormant.

Then, in 1880-81, there was a renewed flurry of activity. Henry Tennant, General Manager of the NER, wrote from York in October 1880 asking the CKPR to provide accommodation at Cockermouth for three NER engines engaged in the coke traffic to Workington. He believed that '…there was an arrangement of this character some time ago.'

Previously, the only real obstacle to the CKPR making the old engine shed available had been the tendency of the LNWR to make use of 'the old workshops and tools'. Now there were other problems. Mr Thompson enlisted the help of George Findlay, at Euston, who was soon to be General Manager of the LNWR. In the meantime, F. W. Webb, the LNWR Locomotive Superintendent, indicated from his Crewe headquarters that he could provide accommodation for two or three NER locomotives at his Workington shed on terms to be agreed, as a temporary measure. However, Mr Tennant made it clear that what he wanted was stabling at Cockermouth – he did not want the extra mileage involved in running to and from Workington. The CKPR therefore asked the Cockermouth joint committee to erect an engine shed for the use of the NER, but its members decided against 'the site in the field adjoining the high level station' (there had been a plan dated November 1878 for such a shed, for NER use) and preferred (May 1881) to use ground recently acquired for extension of the goods station. This itself was not easy, as Mr Senhouse, influential landowner of The Fitz, overlooked the area from his residence and had made it clear that he would not have a locomotive shed on land that he had sold. Mr Wood's plan, as CKPR Engineer, seems to have placed the depot further west and more remote from The Fitz. However, at that time (July 1881) the NER decided to postpone the project. No new locomotive shed was ever built at Cockermouth.

Cockermouth goods shed

Cockermouth has always been a place of varied activities, with an emphasis towards the agricultural community. Thus the railway

One track ran through the goods shed to this eastern (town) end, where an office wing was provided, also stone-built. Observe the continued use of the coal cells ('vaults') in the foreground, in August 1983, 17 years after the railway through Cockermouth closed. *Harold D. Bowtell*

could not postpone indefinitely the provision of an adequate goods warehouse, needed for the transfer of merchandise between railway vehicles and road carts, also for storage, accompanied by offices. A high-powered meeting was held on 1 November 1878 in the Chairman's room at Euston. LNWR Engineer S. B. Worthington presented his plan, estimated to cost £6,900 including about 2½ acres of additional lands. There could be a saving of about £1,000 if the old engine shed were converted into a goods shed.

This modified scheme was agreed, together with extensions of cattle facilities at the upper station yard, where this traffic would be concentrated, while timber would be transferred to the lower station; these rationalisations were effected in course of a few years.

The land required was purchased by the LNWR from Richard Senhouse and his wife for £1,725 under a conveyance of 24 November 1880. For an agricultural site, this sum represented a substantial part of the project's costs. J. B. Worthington made a new road between the railway yard and the river to give Fitz flax mill an access, eliminating the lane behind the old engine shed and the lane's level crossing over the main lines (known as Fitz Road Gate in 1847). This permitted development of the sawmill and timber siding in the north-west and the bringing of a track into the old engine shed from its western end. The stone-built shed was roughly doubled in length, with the extension at the east (or town) end with a single through track, plus internal platform, and a neat office block attached at the east end. The job was done by Mr Boulton, the CKPR's original contractor, for £749 (agreed March 1881). It is interesting today to view this building, well-kept in its present use, with five infilled arches in the south side wall distinguishing the old C&WR engine shed. These may have contained windows in 1847.

Cockermouth yard

The long siding, trailing for westbound trains and maybe dating from 1873-75, would be 'the Stockton siding' for the holding of block loads of coke from the NER, pending breaking up and 'tripping' to Workington Bridge (or beyond) by the LNWR. There were likewise a couple of sidings trailing off the yard line, suitable for holding Up traffic. The yard itself and its buildings changed little after the alterations in hand circa 1881. Timber and Armstrongs' woodyard remained. West Cumberland Farmers handled traffic at the warehouse, and fertilisers became another staple traffic in later days. Decline was rapid under the Beeching policy of 1963; the yard closed wef 1 June 1964, and the whole route through Cockermouth wef 18 April 1966. But the site remains active, served of course by road.

Cockermouth gas works

To avoid carting fuel from the lower yard, the Gas Committee of the Urban District Council proposed a railway siding in 1905-06, but the single track and steep gradient past the works were probable reasons for the CKPR's objections. The connection was not made until LMS days, evidently early in 1928, with the trail-off for Up (ascending) trains and three diverging (east-facing) internal sidings. The sidings were disused by 17 July 1960, and the siding agreement ended on 31 December 1962. The ground frame and trailing lead were removed under authority of January 1963 and the sidings were lifted by August 1964. A proposal (plan) dated 1 March 1915 would have given access more safely, by extending the short siding that trailed off the Up platform line at Cockermouth passenger station. This siding would have paralleled the running line on its northerly side.

Cockermouth joint station, 1865-1966

Development of the site was mainly carried out between the opening to passengers in 1865 and 1881-82. The accompanying plans and photographs give a good idea of this spacious station as it appeared from the 1880s onwards, but with progressive constriction of facilities from the 1930s. The Monday cattle market (supplemented by special sales from time to time) was a salient feature of the town that generated activity virtually all through the life of the railway. By 1882 there were two sidings and 24 cattle pens. Cattle have been

Cockermouth town gas works had long existed, but only secured its railway siding in 1928. The single track on the left climbed from the Junction (for which the Down Distant is in sight) to the passenger station. Working traffic at this siding called for extreme care by operating staff, in view of its direct divergence from a steep single running line with a junction at its foot. *Richard L. Pattinson/CRA*

recalled coming from Ireland, via Silloth and Carlisle, as well as from the mainland. Keswick did not compete.

The main buildings at the passenger station were impressive. The illustrations show them to advantage, as well as the attractive and practical protection provided at the front entrance and on the platform face by the use of glazing. A Boardroom was included until 1869, on the ground floor under the tall gable, with an entrance by way of the station master's garden from the forecourt. The refreshment room was a feature from 1868, when Fred Rapley rented a room. The Whitehaven Cocoa and Coffee House Company put up a purpose-built wooden refreshment room at the east end of the station buildings, completed and occupied from about April 1890. Prominent on many pictures, it closed down circa 1935 and was demolished.

The original single platform proved inadequate and potentially hazardous. An island platform, with passenger access by subway, and an independent Down platform

line and loop platform line, was provided in good time for the concentration of signalling; the signal box of 1875 remained a feature through to 1966. By 1875 there was also a back road to the south of the site of the M&CR's carriage shed, lasting until at least 1934 but removed by 1948. The LNWR carriage siding was elaborated into two roads accommodating a carriage shed – designed, in 1881, to take 12 carriages each 34 feet in length. The shed vanished in LMS days and the surviving siding and loop road to its north were removed under a decision of 1955.

A 42-foot turntable was agreed in principle in 1864 and installed by July 1867, on the Down side at the west end, and may have been the one-time C&WR table from the lower station, which it replaced. It lasted until 1954-55.

Space was always restricted at the Up (east) end, owing to narrowing for the Cocker viaduct, which carried the Up and Down running lines together with a siding on their north side. Notable, eastward, was the steam-driven Tweed Mill of the Cockermouth

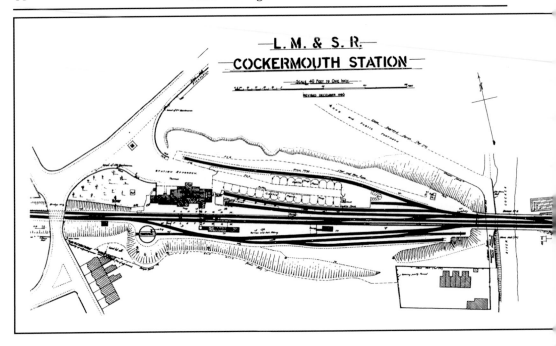

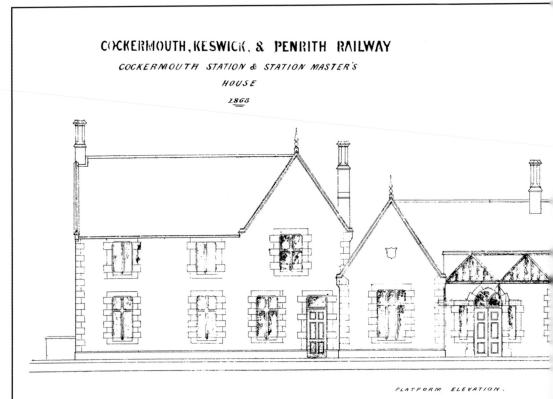

Left Cockermouth station layout

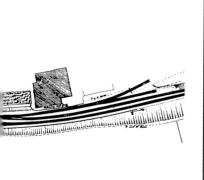

Above A general view of Cockermouth 'joint' station approach and buildings, with the town's war memorial on the right. Cockermouth's fire station now occupies this site. *Harold D. Bowtell*

Left The 1863 architect's elevation of Cockermouth joint passenger station, facing the platform on the Up side of the line. The station master's house is at the left (west) end. On the ground floor, behind the porters' room (the window and door of which are shown here), was a Boardroom entered from the station forecourt. The station master's office was below the gable of the single-storey section, the main entrance was through the double doors from the booking hall, with waiting rooms to the right. *J. M. Hammond collection/Carlisle Record Office*

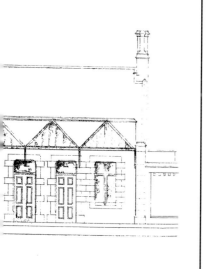

Above A detail view of the entrance porch at Cockermouth passenger station. *David Jenkinson*

Left On a summer morning around the turn of century, Cockermouth folk are smartly turned out; are some perhaps bound for a CKPR Board meeting at Keswick? The handsome refreshment room of 1890, built in timber, has added a prominent east wing to the original buildings. *Roy Anderson collection*

Below left Probably contemporary with the previous view is this picture, from the west end of the station. At the Down platform the LNWR 'Coal Tank' 0-6-2T locomotive is highly polished and in charge of a single coach. The shelter on this platform, and the signal box, can be discerned, as well as the ever-present cattle wagons beyond the refreshment room. *A. G. Ellis collection*

Below A companion view, taken on 7 August 1950, shows LNWR 'Cauliflower' 0-6-0 No 28589 leaving the Down platform with the 10.20am Penrith-Workington train. Staff have been reduced through many economies from circa 1930 onwards and the refreshment room (closed in the 1930s) has disappeared. *E. S. Russell*

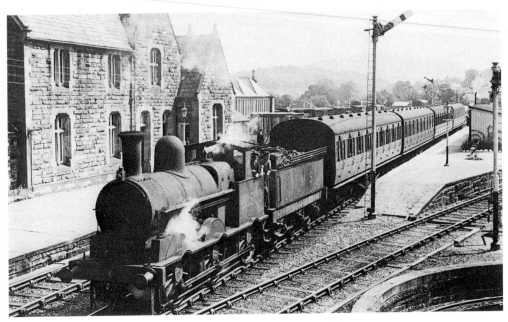

A fine study of Cockermouth station from the signal box on 20 August 1964, as the Up 'Lakes Express' prepares to leave with Ivatt Class '2MT' ('Mickey Mouse') 2-6-0 No 46432. Note the cattle pens on the right. *Derek Cross*

A study of Cockermouth's waiting shelter on the Down island platform. The station was lit by gas provided by the local gas works. Portable steps were provided to help less-agile travellers to board trains. *David Jenkinson*

Cockermouth's small turntable was squeezed in against the embankment at the west end of the island platform. In earlier times NER locomotives hauling mineral trains were turned here. *Richard L. Pattinson/CRA*

Tweed Company, erected 1872-74, for which a siding was approved in May 1872. After 1883 the premises became the Atlas Confectionery Works, and from 1913 cyclecars were made here. In 1919-20 John Hulbert Jnr, of Manchester, demolished the main part of the tweed mill, evidently as an entrepreneurial activity. The CKPR agreed to a private siding, branching off the 'Old Tweed Mill Siding', and were promised 1,000 tons of building stone, derived from the old mill, at 5s9d per ton, bound for Embleton, Braithwaite and Keswick. Oil depots for the Anglo American Oil Company (much later

Esso Ltd) and the Shell Oil Company (Shell Petroleum) took over the use of the sidings east of the river viaduct from 1920 or soon after, and Esso survived there until the end of goods working; a ground frame controlled immediate access. The viaduct was reconstructed between October 1944 and October 1945 and is discussed in more detail in the second volume.

An attractive aspect of Cockermouth station was its tidiness, and as late as 1953-54 it received BR awards. The station nameboards proudly announced 'COCKERMOUTH FOR BUTTERMERE'. Closure was from 1 June 1964 (goods) and 18 April 1966 (passengers).

The town war memorial was placed prominently on the station approach, the site being given by the CKPR under a decision of July 1919, approved by the LNWR, but preliminaries and construction took several years. The memorial stands today, but the station has been totally erased from the landscape. A new fire station building, completed in 1984-85, now occupies the goods yard area.

Staff at Cockermouth

The staff at Cockermouth were, from 1865 until 1922, 'joint' employees; from 1923 they were LMS staff, and BR workers from 1948. The first station master was Joseph Wales, who enjoyed free occupation of the station house to 1870. In that year he was appointed accountant of the CKPR, a career that ended under a cloud in 1885. Mr Mitchell, booking clerk at Cockermouth, became station master, but was given notice in 1881 after a court case. W. Cook followed in that year until he was transferred in 1886 to Greenore, the LNWR terminal in Ireland. R. A. Holt, station master from 1887 to 1891, was removed from office by decision of the Company Secretary. Happily, Robert Little served here successfully from 1891 to 1921. J. W. Ewart (from Embleton, via Bassenthwaite Lake) was appointed in 1921, then promoted to Keswick by the LMS in 1924. The last station master was Thomas Hughes, in 1955-66, following a career in the West Midlands and Furness territory. In 'joint' days the station master was supported by separate booking, parcels and telegraph clerks, as well as a foreman porter and colleagues on the platform.

Joe Carruthers was a regular signalman in the station box from 1936 to 1966, following service in boxes mainly on the West Cumberland coast. Back in 1913 the men in this box were M. Allinson (the senior) and J. W. Stanley, with G. Sanderson (senior) and Joseph Dowthwaite in the Junction box. The senior appointments at the Cockermouth boxes then rated with Keswick A, Threlkeld and Redhills as the best-paid on the CKPR. In earlier days (1872) the sole full-time man in the Junction signal box was on duty daily from about 5.30am until about 10.00pm, with limited relief; no wonder the Board decided to engage a second regular signalman!

4. Embleton to Braithwaite

Climbing from Cockermouth

The C&WR section of the route, terminating in the lower yard at Cockermouth, was essentially a river-level line, but from Cockermouth Junction the CKPR's single line climbed at 1 in 70, flattening after about three-quarters of a mile for the upper station. The resumed single line eastward to Embleton involved a stiff climb at 1 in 75 and 1 in 73, with the prominent farm of Strawberry How on the right, before cuttings and an easing of the gradient to 1 in 150. After Embleton station (2¾ miles from Cockermouth) the gradient fell at 1 in 100 and was then generally level by Bassenthwaite Lake station (3 miles from Embleton) to Braithwaite station (a further 5 miles). Most of these 9 easy miles of railway have been exploited by the road engineers and the new A66 has absorbed the formation.

Embleton station

The station was actually in Lambfoot, but named after nearby Embleton. The single platform was north of the line, its single-storey building having mullioned windows. There was a level crossing at the Up (east) end, with the station master's house (built by Bolton & Graham in time for the opening) on the Up side; the house survives today beyond the crossing. There was never a running loop nor crossing facilities for passenger trains, although, from about the 1890s, tablet instruments were provided in the station office and a goods train could then be stowed in the small yard while a passenger train was handled. Signals were worked from an unprotected ground frame, adjacent to the crossing.

The yard had two short sidings, one serving coal cells, but was extended in, it is thought,

1904, at the request of Mr Bewsher, the local timber merchant, for his sawmill. His successor, T. Rutherford, closed the sawmill in 1926 and the Railway Company removed the connection in 1929. Other railway traffic in timber at Embleton declined in the late 1930s but was livened during the 1939-45 war by the despatch of pit props from Forestry Commission plantations. In 1955 the yard was reduced to just two short sidings, one being occupied by a couple of camping coaches, adapted from LNWR vehicles. The acetylene gas-house was a lean-to structure at the back of the station building and supplied gas for lighting.

A promotional effort in 1906 was the offer of 'golfers' season tickets' between Cockermouth and Embleton, from 1 April to 30 November, for £1 10s (2nd Class) and £1 (3rd).

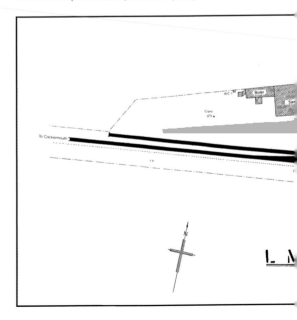

The station closed to all traffic wef 15 September 1958. Plans at that time to transfer the instruments to the east-facing porch of the house, relocate the ground frame on the lawn and convert the platform building as a camping cottage were not carried out. Token exchange was effected right to the end, in April 1966, latterly by the two ladies qualified to operate the instruments, frame and gates, who worked in

Embleton station, with the station master and his staff on the single platform. Also shown are the level crossing at the east end of the platform, the station master's house and the signal post with an arm for each direction. The signalling instruments were in the station office. A66 traffic now sweeps by the site, but the house survives. *A. G. Ellis collection*

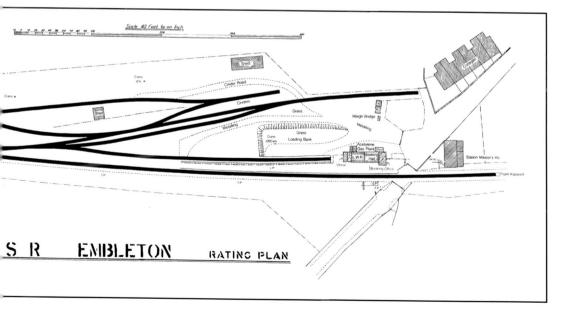

S R   EMBLETON   RATING PLAN

contact with signalmen at Cockermouth and Bassenthwaite Lake.

Rakefoot Crossing

Nearly a mile east of Embleton station a by-road was crossed and a gatekeeper's cottage adjoined; the provision of a station at this point was briefly considered in 1862. There was a tragedy here at an early date (February 1867) when the gatekeeper's wife was killed by a train. Rakefoot was not a block post, but over some years an open frame was used to work the signals, which later were operated by wires connected to the gates. In the 1930s-40s, Tom Sanderson, porter at Bassenthwaite Lake, lived in the house and his wife was gatekeeper, succeeded from about 1946 by their daughter, Mrs Mary Davidson.

Close granite quarry

This quarry was just north of Rakefoot Crossing and the (old) main road. The proprietor, Mr Glossop, was carting his stone to Embleton station in 1908-09, when he first applied for a siding. The connection was actually made in 1912, at a point about half-a-mile east of Rakefoot gates. It was controlled by 'Close Quarry Ground Frame' (dated 1912), always released by the section token and with no cabin or signals. In 1912 the quarry belonged to the Cumberland Granite Co Ltd (proprietor William Spencer, of Skipton, until 1919), the Company becoming Keswick Granite Co Ltd in 1936, also controlling Threlkeld granite quarries, from which men and activity were soon transferred.

Production ended at Close in 1949-50 and activity reverted to Threlkeld. A little railway ballast was seemingly brought out of Close – for transfer to the Engineers Department siding at Keswick by an Up goods train – until effective closure of the siding in 1952. It was derelict by June 1954 and the connection was lifted in 1956.

Narrow gauge tubs ran from the quarry down a self-acting incline to tip into hopper, conveyor, crusher, screens and final hoppers for loading to road or railway wagons. The rail outlet was under the old main road bridge, then by weighbridge and office, over the Dubwath beck and reaching three exchange sidings. An internal-combustion tractor, mounted on rail wheels, figured in the 1930s-40s, propelling wagons (empties) up the grade

The Rakefoot level crossing keeper's cottage, photographed on 17 April 1985 looking roughly westward. The single line passed to the left of the building (the gable end faced the track) and the road seen in the foreground passes over the crossing. The A66 road now occupies the former trackbed in this vicinity. *Harold D. Bowtell*

In the section from Embleton to Bassenthwaite Lake, this access ground frame (left) was released by the token for the section, and the lead trailed off the single line for Up trains to reach the group of exchange sidings and the short private branch to the processing plant of Close quarry. *Richard L. Pattinson/CRA*

to the crusher and loaded wagons from weighbridge to exchange sidings.

Bassenthwaite Lake station

About 1¼ miles from Close Quarry Ground Frame, an eastbound train would run over the level crossing, with attractive signal box to its left, and into the Up platform at Bassenthwaite Lake station – often affectionately known as 'Bass Lake' by railway folk.

While the Up platform never achieved more than a timber structure (albeit featuring waiting and porters' rooms), the Down side had a pleasant single-storey stone building in the general style of those at Embleton and Braithwaite, and provided booking office, general waiting room and ladies' waiting room. This building was flanked to the east by a pair of cottages erected in due course for the two signalmen and their families. To the west was a handsome house for the station master, built by Bolton & Graham contemporary with the station and notable for an attractive internal stairway.

From (seemingly) February 1910 the station master acted also as Sub-Postmaster, and the Railway Company built a Post Office immediately behind the booking office; it was completed in October 1911 and the station master was charged a rent of £6pa for its use.

The station was a crossing place from the start, in 1865, and the Up and Down platform roads were used strictly for movements in the respective directions. A signal box was built in 1874, and electric token instruments, working at that time with Cockermouth to the west

and Keswick to the east, were provided in (probably) 1889. The crossing loops were extended westward of the crossing circa 1899, and later eastward. This latter extension would lead to the installation of the 'auxiliary frame', in a rudimentary small cabin, at the east end of the layout, to work the points (facing for Down trains) at that end. This refinement was completed in December 1902. The same small box remained to control the resited points following a further eastward extension of the loops.

The 'blind' approach by road from the direction of the Pheasant Hotel, south of the level crossing, caused the CKPR board anxiety in the early days of horseless carriages, which were devoid of effective brakes! In 1908 a large 'caution' board was proposed 'to appraise approaching motors of the danger', but on 23 July 1909 Mr Milne's motor car nevertheless sustained damage at the gates. Consequently a proposition was put before the Permanent Way Committee for the installation of a signal on the road, each side of the crossing, to warn drivers of the status of the crossing! The signal was to be 10-12 feet high and designed to operate when the gate locks were bolted. In fact, a larger wheel was installed in the box, to speed gate-opening and closing. Finally, with completion in October 1911, a new signal box was erected closer to the road, giving the signalman better visibility.

The goods yard was behind the Up platform and had four sidings, which were unchanged and well-used for many years by cattle, timber and varied traffic, and of course, coal. There were three coal cells on the back road and

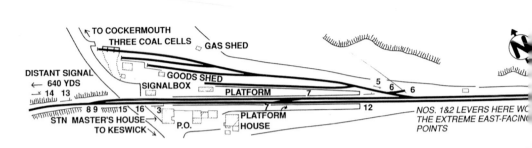

TO COCKERMOUTH

THREE COAL CELLS   GAS SHED

DISTANT SIGNAL
← 640 YDS   ☐GOODS SHED
— × 14 13   SIGNALBOX
              8 9   15 16   3   PLATFORM   7
STN MASTER'S HOUSE→   P.O.   PLATFORM   12
TO KESWICK↘   HOUSE

5 6   6

NOS. 1&2 LEVERS HERE WO
THE EXTREME EAST-FACINC
POINTS

Nos.	RELEASES	LOCKS	BACKLOCKS	Nos.	RELEASES	LOCKS	BACKLOCKS	Nos.
1: DOWN DISTANT			2, 3	7: CROSSOVER ROAD		2,6,12,13		13: UP HOME
2: DOWN HOME	1	7,11,13	16,4	8: UP FACING POINTS	3	9		14: UP DISTA
3: DOWN STARTING	1	7	8,7,16	9: POINT GUARD	13	8		15: WICKET
4: LOCKS FP LEVER IN GF		11		10: SPARE				16: GATE ST
5: SIDING GROUND SIGNAL			6	11: UP ADVANCE	14	2,6,7,4	6,7	GATE WH

NOTE: LEVER No. 11 is released by lever No. 1 in ground frame.

LOCKING DERIVES FROM TWEEDY OF CARLISLE NOVEMBER 15 1902, WHEN SMALL CABIN AND FIRST EXTENSION WAS INSTALLED. SMALL CABIN OR GROUNL

Above The approach to Bassenthwaite Lake station, looking east, as seen from a Penrith-bound diesel multiple unit on 27 July 1963. A green-and-cream-liveried camping coach is glimpsed through the trees on the left. *Preston Whiteley*

Right Station master Jim Airey, resplendent in his uniform, and Mrs Airey are on the Down platform at Bassenthwaite Lake. Note the acetylene gas lamp, and their house. *Jim Airey collection*

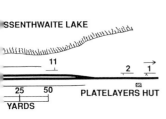

SSENTHWAITE LAKE

11

2 1

25 50 PLATELAYERS HUT
YARDS

RELEASES	LOCKS	BACKLOCKS
14	6,7	9,16
		11,12,13
2,3,13		15

2,3,13 (THESE BACKLOCK THE WHEEL
AND ALSO LEVERS 1 &2 IN GROUND FRAME

CABIN WAS LOCATED 285 YARDS FROM SIGNALBOX.

Above and below Changing seasons at 'Bass Lake', as this station was affectionately known in local railway parlance. The first picture shows a pleasant, sunny day, as three passengers and two railwaymen on the Up platform await the arrival of a Penrith-bound train. Note the colourful flower beds and the neatly trimmed bushes further down the platform. The second view is of a crisp winter's day with plenty of snow. The camping coach (an LNWR-built vehicle) is on the left in this pretty scene. *Both Jim Airey collection*

Above Today the A66 sweeps past 'Bass Lake', whose buildings survive to interest the historian and modeller. In this view Keswick is to the left. *Harold D. Bowtell*

three merchants were represented; after Mealsgate station closed (wef 1 December 1952) a merchant from as far distant as Ireby (6 miles north-eastward) was also installed. Two sidings were taken out in 1951.

To operate the small box the porter on each turn of duty had to walk or cycle out. Often trains crossed, so the station master was hard-pressed to look after both Up and Down trains, and their passengers, simultaneously.

Station masters at this delightful site included Samuel McKenzie (with uniform and house provided) until 1867, John Scott to 1872, William Reay until appointed to Keswick in 1876, Thomas Allison from 1879, John Blackburn in 1908-10, J. W. Ewart from 1910 to 1921 (with later promotion), and Joseph Todhunter from 1921 until his retirement in 1933. Then came Messrs Grimley and Whelan. After the transfer away (circa 1957-58) of Sam Whelan, there was an interregnum and the sub-Post Office was closed. Jim Airey, the last 'Bass Lake' station master (1959-1964) did not have that responsibility. After his time, the station was under the charge of Mr Hughes, based at Cockermouth.

In LMS days Bassenthwaite Lake became, with good reason, a favoured resort for camping coaches, and BR continued this tradition. Before 1939 the vehicles were brought in spring and taken away for overhaul and storage in the winter. In 1959-64 there were two coaches, standing in one of the two surviving short sidings, but the points for this siding were taken out so the occasional move for repair or painting necessitated the temporary slewing of the stabling road into the 'operational' siding.

The gardens, especially on the Up side, were a 'picture', beautifully set against foliage in the summer, with the lake and, beyond it, Skiddaw (3,053 feet) seen ahead, eastward, through a short rock cutting. James Shrives, the Company gardener from Edwardian times until 1921, made 'Bass Lake' his speciality, and Frank Bragg, porter here in the 1920s, was also a particularly keen gardener.

The Reverend Simmons, Secretary and a mainspring of the Friends of the Lake District from the beginnings (in 1934) of this notable organisation, had a special word of praise for Bassenthwaite Lake station and its people. Surely, too, the weekly residents in the camping coaches and the travellers who arrived in early evening by the 'Lakes Express' from London, or left on the last morning of a stay nearby, would echo this pleasure and praise. Closure to goods was wef 1 June 1964, while the station and both signal boxes closed with the line, wef 18 April 1966. The new road sweeps by the surviving station buildings.

Bassenthwaite Lake to Braithwaite
Sir Henry Vane had given land for the railway in the Bassenthwaite Lake station vicinity and he was soon provided with wicket gates and the right to cross the line to his boat landing.

Beyond the rock cutting the line emerged on to the very brink of the lake itself, the formation supported by walls on the left and thus protected from erosion by wind and water. Only half a mile from the station the railway negotiated the point at Castle How, briefly in a cutting with the original main road above it, on the right, supported by massive stone retaining walls and backed by a cliff face. Across the water, on the left, the supremely impressive vista of Skiddaw and its supporting heights opened out.

From MP6¼ to MP9 the line was on a southerly course, then from MP9 to about MP10½ it crossed water meadows to Braithwaite station, 5 miles from Bassenthwaite Lake station. On the waterside section there was a backing (right) by precipitous Wythop woods and the heights beyond. Beck Wythop cottages, a pair built by the CKPR circa 1904 for platelayers, were above the line on the right and are now above the new road. Beyond Powter How, where the meadows were crossed by a low embankment, Thornthwaite village, on the (old) main road in the trees above, was a community that mined and processed lead and zinc. Nearing MP10 an unusual farm lane-cum-aqueduct crossed over the line.

Braithwaite station
This station (which very nearly originated as 'Thornthwaite') was on a curving stretch of the railway route that brought it from north-

to-south to its more familiar west-to-east alignment – and also detaches it from the present-day A66 road, which has usurped its magnificent lakeside course. The gently curving platform was on the Down side of the single line, with a minor level crossing at the Bassenthwaite end. The single-storey stone building had much in common with those at Embleton and Bassenthwaite Lake, with mullioned windows and a steep roof profile, backed in this instance by a substantial stone house, an original structure. The house was extended about 1889 by building an additional room for station purposes behind the waiting room and an additional bedroom above it. With further extensions at the other end, the premises represented a residence of fair size. The staff developed topiary on the Up-side banking, opposite the platform, and a garden beside the platform. In 1954 traveller Eric Hannan remarked on the fine display of roses.

Left The rock cutting at the Up end of Bassenthwaite Lake station, looking back westward to the station, following extension of the loop at this eastern end. 'Bass Lake' provided a crossing facility with ample capacity for lengthy trains. *Richard L. Pattinson/CRA*

Below On Bassenthwaite Lake shore, 'Cauliflower' No 58396 is on the 11.50am Workington-Penrith train of 5 August 1950. This location is south of MP7 (from Cockermouth Junction) and north of the Beck Wythop over-line accommodation bridge and cottages. *E. S. Russell*

Above 'Cauliflower' 0-6-0 No 58389 with the 11.50am ex-Workington duty of 7 August 1950. The train is leaving the southern shore of Bassenthwaite Lake, with railway author O. S. Nock riding on the footplate. Thornthwaite is in the woodlands to the left. *E. S. Russell*

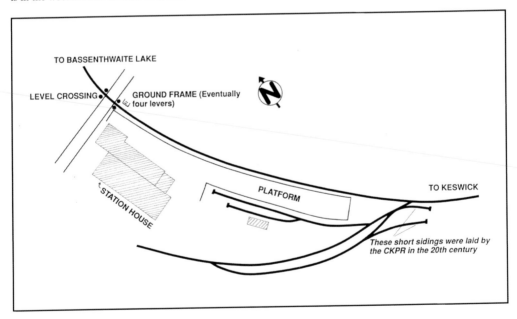

Above Braithwaite station plan

Opposite above On 27 July 1963, looking eastward, the 2.55pm Penrith-Workington DMU enters Braithwaite station. Note the camping coach (right), while on both sides of the line the station gardens are a picture – sadly, to be tended for only two more summers at this stage. This was surely the English country railway at its best. *Preston Whiteley*

Opposite below Another tranquil view, looking west on the same day – a quite delightful sight. *Preston Whiteley*

The goods yard, on the Down side behind the platform, had trailing access for Up trains. In general there were four rather cramped sidings, the two longer (back) ones forming a loop. Minerals figured. Barely a year after opening, the CKPR agreed to build a warehouse for leasing to the Goldscope Mining Company (April 1866), and in the next year (August 1867) agreed to construct a coal depot for the use of G. I. May of the Goldscope Mines. Twenty years on (in April 1887) the Company approved extension of

The substantial house at Braithwaite was built directly behind the station buildings. The CKPR starting signal is shown as a train, still painted in LNWR 'plum and spilt milk' livery, leaves westward. A uniformed member of staff is dividing his attention between despatch of the train (with token) and receiving the lady passenger. He will also have to restore the signals and operate the level crossing gates. *Richard L. Pattinson/CRA*

Happily, the station house and platform buildings at Braithwaite escaped destruction by the road builders and have been well looked after. Here is a study of the detail in the platform buildings, in January 1983. *Harold D. Bowtell*

the shed to accommodate lead ore of the Cumberland Lead Mining Company, with a rental charged.

Thornthwaite Mines Ltd (sometimes, by 1920, using the style 'Threlkeld Lead Mines, Thornthwaite – proprietors Marple & Gillott Ltd, Sheffield') mined lead and zinc from 1873 to 1921 and advertised their operations as 'via Braithwaite station'. Anthony Wilson was Managing Director in 1920. Former footplateman Joe Tinnion, often firing the engine of the Workington-Keswick pick-up goods in 1938-39, recalls that a wagon or two of barytes would often be picked up at Braithwaite, the mineral having come by horse and cart from Newlands Fell. Timber, too, was evident. The LMS (and subsequently BR) installed camping coaches.

Trifling layout extensions were made during the years from 1898 to 1923, with

curtailments between 1948 and 1954, and after, leaving only a siding for the coaches and one (new) short internal loop. Coal sales were evidently handled here from the earliest days, as the station master was dismissed in 1868 for irregularities in the coal business.

As at Embleton, the signals were worked from an unprotected ground frame adjacent to the crossing, and the instruments were in the station office. The electric tablet probably dated from 1893, replaced as elsewhere on the route by miniature token instruments in LMS days. A goods train could be 'locked in' the yard, to allow another train to pass. A second frame appeared in time.

The personnel were reduced and in the last six years of operation (1960-66) there was just one man on each turn of duty, and as this was a block post, he had to be a qualified signalman. Bob Bond, relieving at that time in boxes west of Keswick, remarks that the acceptance and offering on of a train had to be conducted in the office on the platform, after which one crossed to the far side of the line to 'set up the road' before returning to receive the token for the section in rear and give the driver the token for the section in advance. The received staff would be put in the appropriate instrument, the signals restored to danger and maybe the gates opened. There would also be tickets to issue and any merchandise to handle – often crated chickens. The train was then despatched with all customers safe and satisfied, including any arriving visitors or walkers who required directions to the village (half a mile south) or by Whinlatter Pass, up behind Braithwaite, to the Lorton Fells and Loweswater. In quieter moments the signalman refilled the trays of the lighting plant and kept everything tidy. Closure to goods was wef 1 June 1964 and to

passengers wef 18 April 1966, when the railway west of Keswick closed.

Braithwaite to Keswick
It was 2¼ miles from Braithwaite to Keswick by rail. The first mile and a half or so traversed low embankments and a multitude of bridges. In this area Bassenthwaite Lake and Derwentwater threaten to combine from time to time, and this created perpetual and considerable problems for the Railway Company.

Between bridges Nos 45 (Pow Beck) and 47 (River Derwent), the CKPR built Howe Cottages, a pair erected in 1888 on the Down side where a lane crossed by bridge to reach

Right The CKPR identified its bridges by attaching oval cast iron plates of this design. *Author's collection*

Below A 'Cauliflower' approaches bridge No 52 (note the CKPR bridge plate) over the lane near Crosthwaite churchyard. Today the stone abutments carry a footbridge for ramblers. *Richard L. Pattinson/CR*

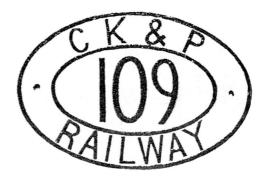

nearby How Farm. The building tender was for £283 13s 0d. The nearest community was in Portinscale. Jack Stamper, ganger in charge of 'the Braithwaite length', lived in one of these cottages during the years before 1940. The houses remain, very pleasant, and one has been extended. Bridge No 47 was the only bowstring girder structure on the CKPR line west of Keswick.

Just beyond the last of the bridges over water, near MP12, St Kentigern's church and vicarage are quietly situated to the south of the railway route. This is Crosthwaite church, which has long played a significant part in the life of Keswick and gained special fame when Canon Rawnsley was the incumbent. The memory of Bishop Eric Treacy is also honoured. In this vicinity today the A66 crosses and recrosses the line of the route. The railway crossed the A591 (to Carlisle) by an under-line bridge and swung briefly south over a lane that developed residentially, and so, by an embankment above Fitz meadows (public park), reached Keswick station.

5. Keswick

A railway headquarters

Workington hid the sea away behind several steelworks. Cockermouth's setting has always been rural rather than rugged. Penrith, too, is a pleasant town, below Beacon Hill, but most of its vistas are distant. Keswick, however, is superbly dominated by lake and mountains; climb gently for a mere 250 feet and the scene is breathtaking.

Keswick has never been a major county or administrative centre, but during 150 years and more it has developed steadily with tourism. The town was pleasantly enlivened by appreciative visitors arriving on its railway, without becoming congested or overwhelmed. Only in the era of the popular motor car and the intrusive motor lorry has it suffered. Since 1972 it has lived without its railway and has instead embraced one of the most hazardous roads in Britain, prominent on the foothills a little to the north of the former station.

Keswick's station was attractive to the eye. It was the headquarters of the CKPR Board of Directors from the 1860s and its discreet development continued under the LMS until 1939. It was quietly businesslike with out-of-season traffic and alive with anticipatory and active bustle several times a day in the holiday season. Its staff established and maintained this air of a headquarters and assumed automatic superiority. They would have it that the 'Lakes Express', bound for London, started here – not from Windermere or Workington, as might be supposed by the uninitiated! In CKPR days the station master donned a top hat and complementary attire to receive Directors and distinguished visitors; some say he wore it whenever on duty.

The passenger station

The lands required at Keswick were purchased from General le Fleming, and the contract to build the station was placed in 1863 with Boulton & Sons, the contractors for the Railway, and was based on a plan presented by Thomas Bouch, the engineer. The alignment was west-to-east, one-third of a mile north of the town centre and with little beyond and above it except the 1,203-foot summit of Latrigg a mile away, with the greater heights of Blencathra and Skiddaw up behind that.

The route was always single line in each direction, but with Up and Down running lines for the length of the platforms, and for a roughly similar distance at the western end, from which direction there was access to the goods yard. The Up passenger platform originally carried only a waiting shelter and (at its east end) a water tank for the use of locomotives. On the Down side a workmanlike stone building of two storeys was built, using local materials. It was well gabled, ostensibly much the sort of building that a comfortably off local Director might have built for his own occupation. As it weathered, against a background of growing trees, and the horse-drawn equipages drew up before its entrance, the analogy would be the more apparent. A glazed 'portico' was added to Bouch's design before construction started. This was a happy touch, affording protection and softening the lines of the building. This building survives today, and may still be studied.

Upstairs, the Boardroom was in the west wing, while the Secretary's office was under the west gable of the centre block. The Traffic Manager's office was under the next gable and the Accountant resided in the east wing.

An impressive view of Keswick, from the slopes of Latrigg, around 1890. The station and hotel are prominent in the foreground, with building work for the island platform in progress. *Valentine*

Above The exterior of Keswick station in later CKPR years; the Company's war memorial plaque is mounted above the post box, under the porch. The old Company's Boardroom was formerly upstairs, in the left gabled wing; its chimney stack is prominent. *Joe W. Brownrigg collection*

Right The original porch canopy at Keswick station was similar to that at Cockermouth. It sheltered many comings and goings and was focal to local life. Here is quite an occasion in the days of the early horseless carriage. At the time, the various hotels' omnibuses would all be horse-drawn. *Author's collection*

Right The LMS substituted a smaller, neat canopy with delicate tracery, although the evidence of the former gabled porch remained on the stonework. *David Jenkinson*

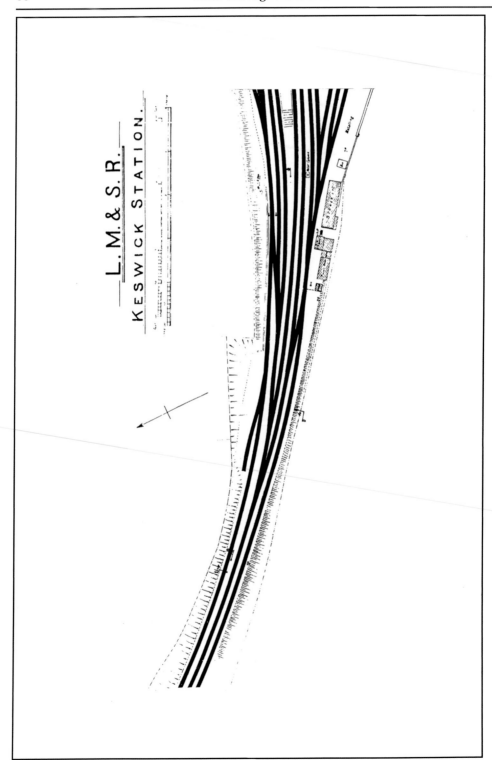

A plan of Keswick, based on the LMS drawing of the 1930s. Observe the alternative sites being considered for the turntable.

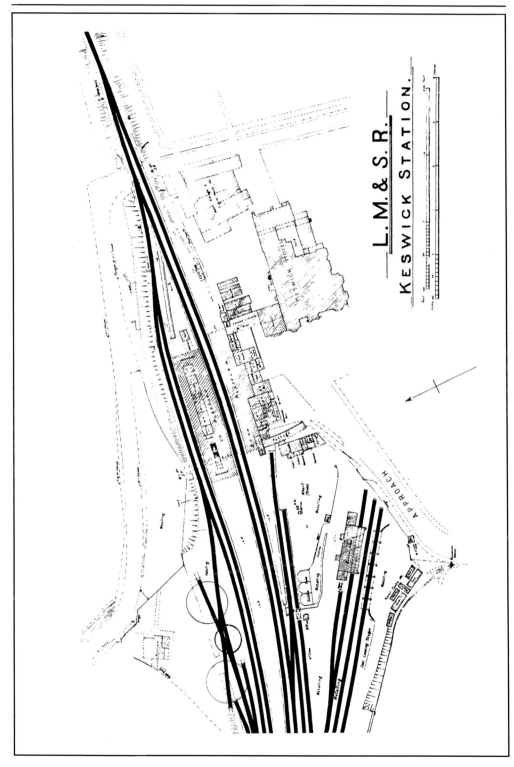

Within Keswick station, in June 1919, the atmosphere of the era is captured by Ken Nunn's shot of No 1675 *Vimiera*, a 6ft 6in 'Jumbo' 2-4-0, on the 11.20am Up passenger from Cockermouth, comprising six-wheeled stock. Through carriages are standing in the short Up bay on the right. Note the ring (uncommon – maybe unique – on the CKPR) on the diverging signal arm, and the brake-van of a Down goods train. In the yard beyond are cattle wagons, pit-props and other timber. *LCGB/Ken Nunn Collection*

The ticket office and usual waiting rooms and other premises occupied the lower floor, opening on to the platform; these were rearranged in the 1890s. The Keswick Hotel (of which more later) was built for the Railway Company in the 1860s, when it was considered to be an essential part of the project; it faces on to the forecourt from the eastern side. Happily, it continues to offer hospitality to visitors.

A surprising aspect was the short life of Keswick station's refreshment room. It opened in 1865 (or very soon after) and was let from the outset to the Hotel Company. Around 1871-72 other parties volunteered to operate the room at higher rentals than the £45-£50 per year being paid. Then, on 8 August 1872, the CKPR Board unanimously agreed that it was desirable to withdraw the refreshment facilities. The Hotel Company acquiesced and it was duly closed by 10 April 1873. One is left assuming, perhaps, that a rowdy and possibly drunken element had caused problems, on days when excursion trains predominated. After closure, a 1st Class gentlemen's waiting room and an additional lavatory were

constructed in the space relinquished (1873) – which itself had been curtailed in 1871 by creating a 2nd Class ladies' waiting room and modifying the lavatories.

Bookstalls

The CKPR Board, which always cast a jealous eye towards Windermere, wished to have a bookstall, selling all newspapers either at their published prices or at least on the same terms as at Windermere. That was in their first year of traffic, in 1865. It is not clear whether any arrangements were made at this time, but in 1869 the matter was taken in hand by Charles Mason, Assistant General Manager of the LNWR. He agreed terms with W. H. Smith & Son for the opening of bookstalls on the stations at Keswick (CKPR), Cockermouth (CKPR/Joint Committee), Workington (by this time, LNWR), and Whitehaven (also LNWR). The arrangements took effect in 1870 or early 1871. The LNWR and W. H. Smith renewed the agreement for this group of bookstalls from time to time, but Smiths declined to continue the arrangements for Keswick and

Cockermouth stations after 31 December 1905.

It was not until February 1909 that the CKPR formally concluded an alternative agreement with Wyman & Sons for the operation of a bookstall (with advertising privileges) at Keswick station, and with Kershaw Ltd for Cockermouth station. By 1914 Wyman ran both bookstalls but Kershaw were permitted to advertise. In January 1921 Wyman may well have taken over the Cockermouth bookstall entirely, but at that time the right to operate at Keswick station had recently been granted to A. Chaplin, stationer, of 19 Station Street, and (in line with current LNWR practice) advertising rights at the station were secured by Frank Mason & Company, of Maxwell House, Arundel Street, Strand, London. Around 1931 Wyman again took over the bookstall (and kiosk on the island platform) at Keswick (from Chaplins) but closed down the bookstall during the 1950s. Wymans closed Cockermouth bookstall circa 1961.

Keswick's well-known subway

It was decided in 1873 to build the subway, which became a familiar feature of Keswick station, linking the platforms and also providing direct access to and from the forecourt by way of a passage with a glazed roof.

The prominent water tank

The water tank for locomotives, at the east end of the Up platform, dated from 1864, but was reconstructed and enlarged under a contract of July 1880 with Cowans, Sheldon & Company, of Carlisle. This tank was prominent through to the closure of the station in March 1972, with Cowans, Sheldon's number 44 and date 1880 carried upon it.

Expansion and improvements in the 1890s

Whereas most daily trains ran through to and from Workington, the excursions normally terminated at Keswick towards noon and had to start homeward at early evening. The engines and carriages had meanwhile to be accommodated. Increasingly, too, through carriages were kept overnight at Keswick and attached to popular trains in the morning. Thus resources became overstrained.

A loop line had been laid behind the Up platform by 1889, when lengthening of that loop at the west end (and laying in of a second loop, behind it) were also proposed. For these developments a strip of land was purchased from Mr le Fleming, owner of the adjoining field. Between 1890 and 1893 development was carried out progressively, bringing the passenger station and its layout to essentially the form known during the ensuing 70 years, with Board of Trade inspection of the virtually completed works taking place on 2 November 1894. The Up platform was moved back somewhat and reconstructed as a lengthy island, broad in its central portion. This permitted slewing of the main Up and Down running lines and the widening of the Down

A pleasant portrait of Keswick's distinctive water tower, at the eastern end of the island platform, and the attractive buildings. *Peter W. Robinson*

Above An Ivatt '2MT' 2-6-0 of
12D (Workington) shed calls at
Keswick on 20 August 1964 with
the Down 'Lakes Express'. The
glazed screen design of the island
platform buildings is shown to good
effect. *Derek Cross*

Below No 46432 leaves Keswick
with the 'Lakes Express' in July
1964, seen from the western end of
the station and included to show the
bay platform layout and loading
gauge. *Harold D. Bowtell*

platform by about 7ft 6in, in front of the station
buildings, accomplished in 1894-95. Behind
the island another platform track took the form
of a long loop, subsequently parallelled by a
second long loop, suitable either for running
engines round their stock, or stabling a train. A
short bay road was provided at the Up end of
the island and a bay in the western end of the
main Down platform. Handsome glazed roofing
was installed over a substantial part of both
platforms, and there was a range of attractive
timber buildings on the island, which featured
free-standing glazing.

A locomotive turntable was installed near
the boundary of the site, as extended a little
northward, behind the station. It was probably
at this period when the Down platform was
lengthened at its east end by a narrow timber
extension. This proved a source of trouble in
the prevailing climate, being found decayed
and unsafe in 1919, and likewise in 1946.

Electric light

Opportunely, within a few years of the
completion of these improvements, which
aided railway operating and the comfort of

travellers, there came the offer by the Windermere & District Electricity Supply Company to install electric lighting. The company undertook to provide a regular supply of electric current, and their tender of £303 for a comprehensive installation was accepted in November 1899. In view of the early date, and this being the only station on the CKPR route (except Penrith, and that in recent times) ever to benefit from electric light, the initial list of lamps is quoted, slightly summarised:

Upper floor: Board room: four drop lamps, each of 8cp (candle-power); Secretary's office: two drop lamps of 8cp and one lamp of 25cp; Clerks' office: five drop lamps of 16cp; Accountant's office: four drop lamps of 16cp.
Ground floor of the main buildings: Station entrance: one lamp of 50cp and two outside lamps of 16cp each. Booking office (Down): four lamps of 16cp each; Station master's room: one lamp of 16cp.
Island platform and associated rooms: Booking Office (Up Platform): three lamps of 16cp, one being outside; Station master's office (Up): two lamps of 16cp. (There were also lamps in other rooms on the island platform, and in the subway.)
Signal box 'B' (on Down platform): two lamps of 16cp.
Signal box 'A' (westward): two lamps of 16cp.
Workshop and offices: eight lamps of 16cp.
Goods warehouse: two lamps of 16cp.
Goods office: two lamps of 16cp.
Goods yard: two arc lamps.

Any reader who can recall the dim glow from a carbon-filament electric bulb of 25 candle-power, deriving power typically at 110 volts dc from public generation, would not have been overwhelmed by the brilliance of Keswick station and yard as the new century approached.

Before completion of Keswick station and hotel, in the 1860s, the CKPR planned to take gas from the Keswick Gas Company. One is left doubting whether this supply materialised for the station and goods yard, as the prospect of electricity was seized upon without hesitation.

Hydraulic power
In 1900, a hydraulic lift was installed between the Up (island) platform and the subway and another in the Keswick Hotel. The water came from the lands of Mr Spedding – who was Chairman of the Railway Company's Board – but his farm needs were paramount. By February 1902 there was concern at the inadequacy of the supply in times of drought. An engine and hydraulic pump were installed, the cost being shared, two-thirds by the Hotel Company and one-third by the CKPR. In the 1930s, when Roy Hughes was the LMS engineer responsible for the CKPR section, he encountered problems with this supply. The farmer modernised his operations by installing a milk cooler – which promptly took all the water, necessitating a long period of diplomacy and pipe-cleaning to secure the needs of hotel and railway.

Telephones
Another refinement was the telephone, provided by the National Telephone Company, whose business passed to the Post Office in 1912. The first instrument was placed in the Company's office (upstairs), along with one in the station master's office (downstairs), in 1910. In the following year extensions were made to the goods and parcels departments – following upon representations by tradespeople.

Later changes
A shed for bicycles and luggage was placed at the west end of the Down platform in 1913, while in 1914 some modification of Down-side waiting rooms seems to have followed. Eventually a plain glazed roof was substituted for the decorative portico, but the LMS superimposed quite an attractive and airy structure bearing the name 'Keswick'. Following some previous use of light-coloured paintwork, the station was finished in green and cream, around 1960.

Keswick goods station
Unlike its passenger counterpart, the goods station at Keswick was positively and honourably parochial. The eastbound ironstone (or empties) and coke (westbound)

all passed it by, the trains pausing only long enough for their engines to take water or enlist assistance in the rear.

The yard was at first tucked neatly into a near triangular site. On its south side was a coal road, traversing seven coal cells. One track passed through the stone-built goods shed, laid between the coal road and a short siding that terminated just short of the building. Finally, there were two fairly long sidings close to the Down running line, one of which came alongside a loading bank, or platform, with a 5-ton capacity crane handy. The yard tracks converged into the Down running line (without a headshunt) just before it joined the Up line – and there was also a siding on the north of the site.

All major changes in the yard were made before the end of the 19th century. A short stage (platform) was built beside the approach line to the coal cells, to ease discharge of side-door wagons. The neat and matching goods office was added circa 1877 to the west end of the shed, and the short track was cut back to accommodate it. The loading bank acquired three cattle pens and the track next to the running road became effectively a bay platform line. Significant, however, was a widening of the formation, westward, circa 1880, and the creation of a useful headshunt. This permitted the shunting of all roads in the yard without fouling the running line.

A weighbridge for railway wagons eventually appeared on the line beside the loading bank and this probably derived from the demands away back in 1880 of the traffic from the Buttermere Green Slate Company. Just inside the road entrance was a weighbridge for carts and lorries; beside it stood a charming weighhouse, in vertical timbering with slated roof and tall, decorative finial, presenting the air of a pagoda in north Lakeland.

A relatively late development was the provision of a small oil store, near the southern boundary of the yard, left of the road entrance. The Anglo American Oil Company (much later becoming Esso) and the British Petroleum Co Ltd (BP) were both permitted to establish their first stores in 1912.

Signal cabins and workshops

A Saxby & Farmer brick signal box, with slated roof, hipped at the ends, was built in

A view into Keswick goods yard from Station Road. The timber-built weighbridge cabin was of a pagoda-like design, with the stone-built goods shed beyond. Today a leisure centre occupies the yard site. *David Jenkinson*

The track entering the western end of Keswick goods shed is obscured, but Percy Sanderson's one-time office is shown. The coal cells are beneath the right-hand siding, which is designed for the discharge of NER bottom-door wagons. *David Jenkinson*

1874 on the Down side near the yard outlet. This brought together the operation of most of the running line points and signals, as well as giving the signalman an oversight of shunting movements. A quaint little signal cabin was provided on the Down platform, towards its east end, in (probably) 1889; it was superseded by a new box in 1932. The 1874 box became 'Keswick A', while the 1889 box became 'Keswick B', although in LMS days the styling was No 2 and No 1 respectively. The woodwork of both boxes was painted green and cream by the 1960s.

Workshops and stores (single-storey brick buildings) were clustered close behind the 'A' box, originally accommodating the CKPR's joiners, plumbers and blacksmith, who shoed the Company's horses, amongst other work. The stables were to the right, when entering the yard gates, and eventually a garage was added to the block.

Traffic in Keswick yard

Coal was always the major inward traffic. Prior to 1923 fuel for CKPR stations was primarily an NER responsibility and, accordingly, bottom-door wagons were used. The staff liked them, for side-door wagons – sometimes received from pits via Brayton (M&CR), Whitehaven or Workington way, and occasionally from Durham or Yorkshire pits – called for much shovelling. The town gas works was a regular coal customer, with one cell reserved; they sent their own lorries, which reversed in for loading. Other cells were rented by merchants, who bagged their coal as required and undertook their own cartage to customers.

A staple outward traffic by rail was slate from the Buttermere Green Slate Company's Honister quarries, certainly back to the early 1880s and probably before that. The Company not surprisingly undertook its own cartage of the prized slate, using two-wheeled carts for a long period, each pulled by a single horse, over the hilly route to Keswick. Before the 1914-1918 war a steam lorry was sharing the job. By the 1930s a Sentinel steam lorry was employed by the quarries on the run to Keswick station. There had been talk of a link

Keswick No 2 signal box, a Saxby & Farmer structure built in 1874. The single-storey brick building to the rear was the CKPR's joiners and plumbers workshop. *David Jenkinson*

by steam light railway – and quite some railway it would have been – and this is touched upon later.

Timber merchants, with their own sawmills in Keswick, delivered wood by road to the station yard for despatch by rail. Pit props were sent mainly to West Cumberland. There was also wood bound for the short run by rail to the Briery Bobbin Mill's siding. Keswick was proud of its two pencil manufacturing mills, amalgamated in 1912 and reduced by one from about 1939. The railway carters collected their consignments. There are still pencils made in Keswick by the Cumberland Pencil Company.

The West Cumberland Farmers' Trading Society maintained a depot at Keswick, receiving supplies by rail. In autumn the Railway sought orders from the farmers round about – to load sheep for despatch to winter pastures, often via Gretna, and to bring them back in the spring.

Traffic for NER destinations was consigned to Penrith or Carlisle for transshipment, or for onward transit if in full wagon loads.

The siding at the west end of Keswick, on the north (Up) side, was lengthened westward some time during the first 20 years of this century. In LMS days it was favoured for the stabling of Engineers Department wagons of railway ballast, from Close quarries at Embleton.

Keswick carts and carters

In October 1866, well over a year after opening, the CKPR decided 'to purchase a lurry, horse, etc, in order to execute the Company's cartage work at Keswick', and in May 1867 the purchase of a second horse was authorised. Joseph Tinnion was the carter, but he was promoted to Foreman Porter at Keswick in 1867, and Mr Fearon, a platelayer, took the carter's job from August of that year. Isaac Atkinson succeeded as 'cartman' at Keswick, his pay being increased in May 1873 from 19 to 20 shillings (£1) per week. By November 1877 the lurry (a spelling maintained by some Railway Companies until the 1920s!) was worn out and replaced. There was only one horse in these times, and nine years on it was reported 'too old' and another was purchased. Similarly, in April 1907, a horse was superannuated and replaced.

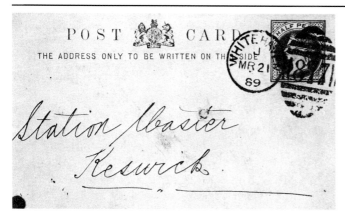

Left and below Traffic destined for Keswick in the late 19th century was indeed varied. On notification cards despatched to William Reay (CKPR station master from 1876 until his death in 1908) is recorded a range of merchandise from fenders to straw and sugar. This example was posted from T. R. Metcalf, of Tangier Street, Whitehaven, on 21 March 1889 and carried a halfpenny stamp. The message reads: 'Please deliver 3 bags sugar ex Liverpool consigned to my order to W. Thomas Barnes, Grocer, Keswick.' *J. M. Hammond collection*

A further selection of consignment instructions for station master Reay includes (*right*) five barrels of 'petroleum oil' for Mr W. Dunbobbin, of Keswick, from The Kerosene Company, Fazakerley Street, Liverpool. The delivery order from Baxendale & Company, Miller Street, Manchester (*above middle*), requests the delivery of six garden seats to Mr J. H. Smith of Skiddaw Lodge, Keswick, while the third (*above*) records the delivery to Keswick of one barrel of tar for the company's own use. *All J. M. Hammond collection*

William Greenhow, the CKPR Keswick carter, is in town in April 1917 with his horse and heavy-duty Company cart, collecting waste paper for sale in aid of the local military hospital, established in Lord Rochdale's home of Lingholm. This collection was the initiative of Mrs George Hogarth, and the family shop appears. *Fitz Museum collection*

Two horse-drawn carts were maintained by the summer of 1913, when an increase in wage levels led to carter W. Greenhow receiving a pay rise from 23 to 24 shillings weekly. His colleague Fleming Barnes was advanced from 22 to 23 shillings for a week's work. Mr Greenhow drove the four-wheeled cart used for the heavier deliveries while Mr Barnes was in charge of the parcels cart, said also to have four wheels but of lighter build, with a detachable cover. The two carts comprised the fleet in the CKPR's later years, from 1920 to 1922, when Jack Tyson was one of the carters. It is believed that the carts remained in use for some years after this; the carters worked from 7.30am until 4.00 or 5.00pm.

Rather surprisingly, during the war, in September 1915, the Company considered introducing motor traction for the delivery of goods at Keswick, but this was not pursued and new stables were built instead. In July 1919 a scale of charges was compiled for delivery of parcels beyond a 1-mile radius from Keswick station. In general, delivery was not charged to Chestnut Hill or The Forge, towards Penrith, nor to Portinscale, about a couple of level miles in the opposite direction. Eventually a motor vehicle replaced the parcels cart and its horse, and the new vehicle undertook longer journeys, for a fee. A garage was built on to the southern end of the stable block, as indicated by a drawing of 1946. Finally, there were two motor vehicles and their drivers. In 1953

reconstruction of the stable, to accommodate two motors, was proposed.

The locomotive turntable

At the planning stage, in November 1863, a turntable and a shed for one engine were proposed, together with a shed for six (small) passenger carriages. The LNWR, which undertook to provide locomotives, carriages and train crews, did not require the CKPR to provide engine or carriage sheds at Keswick and none were ever built there. The turntable was implicitly of early date. On 2 June 1914, doubtless the day after the Whit Monday Bank Holiday and with excursion traffic still at a peak, a girder of the table was broken while turning an NER locomotive. The Cowans, Sheldon Company, of Carlisle, was invited to tender for the repair.

As the LMS programme for strengthening of bridges progressed through the 1920s and 1930s, the time approached for the running of more powerful locomotives through from the main line to Keswick, and the inadequacy of the turntable had to be faced. The relevant drawing came from the Chief Engineer, then based at St Pancras, dated 12 July 1938, and showed the replacement of a 40-foot diameter turntable by one of 60 feet. It was vacuum-operated and sited just west of the old table, its well extending into the field between the former northern boundary of the railway territory and the detached house provided for the station master. Connection was to the 'Jubilee Road', namely the back loop line beyond the platform loop, and, like the old table, it could be reached from either west or east. It is generally recalled in railway circles as being completed around the end of 1939, or early in 1940. The LMS drawing of the works is dated 1940, showing the new connections. However, contemporary reports are clear that the new turntable was first used commercially on Saturday 24 June 1939, and that Stanier 'Black 5' 4-6-0 locomotives worked the summer Sunday expresses from Glasgow and Newcastle-upon-Tyne to and from Keswick on the immediately ensuing Sundays, and were turned. There was little demand for turning Class '5', '5X' and '6' 4-6-0 engines during the war years from autumn 1939, nor indeed during the following years, so this handsome table saw comparatively little use and (although retained in a review of 1963) was taken out of use before April 1966, when the last trains ran west of Keswick on the route. At the time of writing, the turntable well can still be viewed as a monument to what might have been.

The approach and environment at Keswick station

The CKPR ordered its contractors to construct an approach road to its station at Keswick; the road was straight, broad for its day and impressive, with a bridge over the Greta river and a concluding sweep past the goods yard gates to reach the spacious forecourt shared by both station and hotel. Its conception was worthy of a headquarters. The bridge was of 60-foot span over the river, in cast and wrought iron, with a secondary 20-foot stone arch (sidespan), the whole structure being widened in the 1890s or soon afterwards. In 1890-93 a diverging road was made, passing behind the hotel at a lower level, to afford access to the coach houses and stables and continuing through the under-line bridge east of the station to reach the station master's dignified house. This was built to the designs of architect Mr Ross, of Carlisle, the builder being R. Harrison, under contract of March 1865; a bathroom was added in 1912 and the house still stands today. Across the

road was the estate of John James Spedding, of Greta Bank, a CKPR Director from 1861 to 1909, and Major Spedding in succession.

The residents of Chestnut Hill, on Keswick's higher eastern outskirts, soon called for a short-cut to the station, and in 1873 the Railway was prepared to contribute to the cost, but it was not until 1898 that a committee (helped by £20 from the CKPR) had a suspension-type footbridge built over the Greta. This provided a pleasant footway from the Penrith road, near Millfield House, to the CKPR's back road round the hotel. Also in 1898 it was decided to make an inclined path from this back road to the Down platform; regrettably neither the bridge (abandoned since the railway closed) nor path exist today.

Station Road and the road round the hotel were subjects of periodical debate. In 1876 the Railway decided not to dedicate these roads to the public, and in the 1880s a chain and temporary gate was placed across Station Road, suitably manned, on one day each year. Presumably only bona fide travellers were permitted through, on sufferance! On 1 January 1904 platelayers Joseph Little and Thomas Gibson held a chain across the road, between two stone boundary posts, from 8.00am to 5.00pm, and this procedure was applied again on Monday 2 January 1905 and subsequently. Its revival coincided with a period of irritation with Keswick Urban District Council, who were pressed by the Company during 1900 to take over the roads – and especially the Greta bridge – in accordance with the Railway's interpretation of an early agreement. The Council declined. In fact, the bridge remained as Railway property until its sale (with the station) to the Lake District Special Planning Board some years after the railway's closure.

In addition to being primarily a route to the station and hotel, the Station Road in time also gave access to benefactions received by the town of Keswick. Higher Fitz Park, with its gates dated 1882, was developed to the east of the road on land bought from the Keswick Hotel Company, and the Fitz Trust also laid out Lower Fitz Park (on land acquired from the le Fleming family) on the road's west side. This too was opened in the early 1880s and

This view takes us back to Keswick circa 1868. The Greta river bridge and Station Road have been newly constructed, as has all else seen here. Note the coal cells in the left distance and the goods shed behind them, with wagons and derrick crane, the tall signal and the main station building (already with its porch). The Keswick Hotel is as yet unfinished, with no conservatory or covered way yet evident. *Fitz Museum collection*

boasts gates (erected circa 1898) 'in memory of J. S. Crossthwaite' (a prominent early Fitz Trustee). The Keswick (Fitz) Museum, nearing the station on the west side, is of 1897, and its northern wing, of 1905, is the art gallery 'in memory of T. & H. Hewetson, 1897'. The museum and gallery are happily cared for and quietly improved as the years go by. Henry Hewetson (1821-95) never forgot his boyhood in Keswick and Hewetson funds endowed several of these projects.

In the first year of passenger traffic (1865) Edmund Grayson wished to place a drinking fountain on the road near the station. The fountain, designed for people and dogs, is still there today, in the right-hand wall of Station Road, on entering from the town. It can be seen before the bridge, and is inscribed 'IN MEMORY OF FRANCES ROLLESDON 1865 Whosoever drinketh of the water that I shall give him shall never thirst. *John IV 14.*'

Close at hand is a memorial stone placed in 1923 by Mr & Mrs J. B. Wivell, of the Keswick Hotel, in memory of their son, George Banks Wivell, and daughter, Mary Wivell. There is also a stone of November 1939 in appreciation of Dr R. K. B. Crawfurd, JP.

Hotel omnibuses

The residential hotels of Keswick gained most of their business from visitors, who arrived by train at the station. The 'Keswick' soon had direct access, but all the others were at a considerable distance. Thus, in general, each commissioned a smartly turned-out horsed omnibus to meet arriving trains, convey anticipated guests and encourage support. Around 1903 the Railway Company sought to ease the resulting congestion by delineating individual stands – one might say 'parking' or 'waiting' places – in return for a fee. By 14 January 1904 all were allocated for the year and contention resulted, and recurred over the years.

One notes, for example, that in October 1911 Mr Messenger was permitted to place a

This was the sight that greeted many travellers arriving at Keswick by train. As they stepped out from beneath the glazed porch there was a row of smartly turned out horse-drawn buses owned by the local hotels. *Joe W. Brownrigg*

char-a-banc on his last omnibus stand, adjoining the covered way. It could have been a horse or motor vehicle, and would in either case be an open coach, with forward-facing leather bench-type seats, rising in tiers towards the back, as in a theatre, so that every passenger might have an uninterrupted view of the scenery. The vehicle would be used for a 'round tour'.

Omnibuses for a short station-to-hotel run usually conveyed their passengers inside, with their backs to the side windows and a centre aisle, while the roof carried trunks and other luggage, flanked by railings and upper side boards proclaiming the name of the hotel. Towards the end of the CKPR's independence, the omnibus stands at Keswick station were let for the year 1921 as follows:

1.	Pape's Coaches Ltd, Royal Oak & Queen's Hotels	£47
2.	J. H. Fletcher, lodging houses	£17
3.	J. Boadle, King's Arms	£4
4.	Pape's Coaches Ltd, George Hotel	£2
5.	Pape's Coaches Ltd, Blencathra and Park	£1
6.	H. T. Pape, Lodore Hotel	£1
7.		
8.	T. C. Stanley, Derwentwater Hotel	£1
9.	J. Wilson, Lake Hotel	£1
10.	J. Young, cab	£2
11.	Pape's Coaches Ltd, Skiddaw and County	£3
12.	W. D. Wivell, cab or taxi	£5
	Total	£84

Representation of hotels

Railways were traditionally jealous of their right to restrict access to platforms, but the CKPR used to allow a select few representatives of hotels on to the platform to meet passengers. For example, in 1912 the annual fee was £12 10s, and only four subscribers were accepted: Mr Messenger (Keswick Hotel), Mr J. S. Harker (Lodore Hotel), Mr D. N. Pape (Royal Oak Hotel), and Mr T. C. Stanley (Derwentwater Hotel). By the 1930s only the Keswick Hotel was allowed to place a representative on the platform, dressed in his distinctive uniform.

Royal visitors

The German Kaiser Wilhelm called at the Keswick Hotel for tea in August 1895 and there exists a classic picture that includes his carriage outside the hotel entrance.

On 17 October 1956 the Queen (who also visited the Keswick Hotel) was photographed on the station platform, under the canopy. This would be the occasion that caused concern in railway circles; the party had travelled by car from West Cumberland and was about 20 minutes late at Keswick, with consequent delay to the Royal Train, which started from there. Another Royal Train, of limited load, came down from Penrith on 22 July 1966.

The ambulance challenge shield

Ambulance work, on a voluntary and spare-time basis, has always been supported enthusiastically by railwaymen, with accommodation and encouragement offered by the railways. The CKPR's ambulance teams competed for a shield. It is good to know that the competitions continue today, the 'Keswick' shield being on display from year to year at places as far apart as Carlisle and Morecambe, the competing teams being drawn from a wide area.

The CKPR ambulance challenge shield. The inscription on the lower part of the shield reads: 'Presented by the Directors for annual competition by employees. Henry Howard Esq, Chairman, 1914.' It was competed for originally within the territory of the CKPR, but it has since figured as an award of standing in a much wider railway territory. *Harold D. Bowtell*

An occasion to be remembered was on Sunday 22 May 1966. A parade of the St John Ambulance Brigade for annual inspection took place in Keswick and an impromptu bandstand was created when the band proceeded via the station subway and played on the island platform, with the appreciative audience standing on the main Down platform. That was during the short period while Keswick was a terminal station but before it was reduced to a single operational platform. The prevailing weather is better not recalled!

Barrow and spade

The inscription engraved on the handsome spade, accompanied by a wheelbarrow of carved magnificence seen in the accompanying illustration, reads 'PRESENTED TO T. A. HOSKINS ESQ, JP, ON THE OCCASION OF HIS CUTTING THE FIRST SOD OF THE COCKERMOUTH KESWICK & PENRITH RAILWAY MAY 21 1862.'

Thomas Alison Hoskins, of High Hall, near Cockermouth, was the first Chairman of the CKPR Board, holding the office from 10 August 1861 until his resignation on 2 November 1867. His term embraced the period of practical decisions, the construction of the line and its opening to traffic in November 1864, fully effective by January 1865. The memorial wheelbarrow and spade were duly held by T. A. Hoskins until about 40 years after the opening, when his son, Colonel R. Hoskins, of Fairfield, Pencraig, Ross-on-Wye, wrote on 30 January 1905 to Sir Henry Vane to offer these mementos. They were received by the Railway's Board by 25 February 1905 and it is understood that they were displayed in or near the Boardroom. On 10 March 1923, when the LMS was already in being and the CKPR Board were winding up their affairs, they determined to offer the barrow and spade to the Fitz Park Museum. The Museum trustees and curator still prize these items, which are beautifully kept and worthily displayed.

'In Proud and Honoured Memory'

'COCKERMOUTH KESWICK &
PENRITH RAILWAY COMPANY
IN PROUD & HONOURED MEMORY OF
THE EMPLOYEES OF THIS COMPANY
WHO GAVE THEIR LIVES FOR
KING & COUNTRY IN
THE GREAT WAR
1914-1918

Wm NOTMAN, Sergeant, Border Regiment
J YOUDALE, Corporal, Border Regiment
J GIBSON, Private, Border Regiment
JW HEBSON, Private, Border Regiment
WP HETHERINGTON, Private, Border
    Regiment
MS MITCHINSON, Private, Border
    Regiment
R WATSON, Private, King's L'pool Regiment'

Here, in Keswick's Fitz Museum on 22 February 1983, are the handsome spade and barrow used in 'turning the first sod' for the CKPR on 21 May 1862. *Harold D. Bowtell*

This is the inscription on the copper plaque that was produced at the wish of the Board of the CKPR. The tracing of the design was approved on 20 September 1919 and the tablet was engraved in the Keswick School of Industrial Arts, which incidentally owed its foundation to Canon and Mrs Rawnsley. It was affixed to the front wall of Keswick station, beside the entrance and above the post box (which is still in situ and in use). It faced the southerly sun and gained weather protection from the entrance canopy.

The tablet was unveiled publicly on 1 May 1920 by Major Hamlet Riley DL, JP, LLB (Cantab) (1851-1922), who was then Chairman of the Railway Company. He died in office on October 1922 after 31 years on the Board, and was the last formal Chairman of the CKPR.

Somewhat before the closure of Keswick station, on 6 March 1972, the plaque was removed and, thoughtfully, installed on the town's war memorial in the gardens beside the entrance to Station Road. Unfortunately the only available side of the memorial faced away from most beholders, and towards the sunless north. The result has been a sad deterioration by weathering and oxidisation, and it is certainly not a worthy object as seen today. It could doubtless be far better prized and displayed in the great hall of the National Railway Museum at York but, for me, the ideal location is available in Keswick, close to its railway home of some 50 years. This is the Fitz Museum, where it could, after cleaning with the care accorded to works of art, be worthily displayed in a dry atmosphere, perhaps behind glass, along with the memorial barrow and spade and other mementos of the CKPR and its people.

Closure at Keswick

Goods traffic at Keswick ceased wef 1 June 1964. The route westward to Cockermouth and Derwent Junction (Workington) closed to all remaining traffic wef 18 April 1966. From 4 December 1967 operation east to Penrith No 1 signal box was on a 'one engine' basis (which could equally mean one railcar set), the signal boxes at Keswick and intermediately closing. The station was unstaffed wef 1 July 1968, and final closure took effect from 6 March 1972.

The Keswick Hotel

Before the CKPR was open its Board decided that it was imperative to have a 'Station Hotel' at Keswick, and arranged visits to hotels at Grasmere, Windermere and Ullswater on the Lakes tourist 'round'. Mr Ross, the Company's architect, produced drawings, which were approved. Three acres of land were purchased from General le Fleming and in December 1863 the building tender of £8,800, by David Hall, of Carlisle, was accepted. Work proceeded apace and by 1865 an impressive pile resulted. In March of that year the name Keswick Hotel was adopted, furnishing was put in hand and laying out of the grounds was entrusted to Mr Kemp, of Birkenhead. The covered way between station and hotel, such a distinctive

The grand portal of the Keswick Hotel, where HM Queen Elizabeth II has visited and, once, Kaiser Wilhelm called for tea. The hotel entrance is illustrated on 31 August 1982. *Harold D. Bowtell*

This is the covered way that once linked station and hotel and was probably designed as a gravelled path to steps leading to an external side door, but elaborations soon followed. Here, from 1940 to 1945, Roedean schoolgirls and their mistresses held umbrellas to protect them against the rain coming in through leaky roof-lights. Also viewed on 31 August 1982. *Harold D. Bowtell*

feature down the years, was to be constructed. On 1 July 1865 the opening of the railway was celebrated (retrospectively) together with that of the hotel (a little prematurely). The hotel was probably not complete until 1866-67; indeed, the gilded date above the main entrance records 1869.

The Railway Company would have liked to hand over the hotel and its operation to professional hoteliers, and between March and May 1865 the Cumberland Lake District Hotel Company came on the scene, with ambitious plans for the purchase and running of the hotel, and establishment also of a hotel at Bassenthwaite Lake. However, they soon withdrew from the latter project and the Railway lost confidence and created a 'Keswick Hotel Company' as a subsidiary or associate of the CKPR, from 1866, with a common chairman, Isaac Fletcher, from that year. There was a formal contract, under which the Hotel Company were required to purchase the establishment at Keswick. It is noted that, in 1869, they were paying interest charges to the CKPR, evidently on the capital

cost of the building and furnishing and laying out the grounds. The hotel was under lease in those early years, but a conveyance was prepared in 1871.

The story of the hotel soon became linked with the Wivell family. Joseph Banks Wivell, once in the pencil trade, married Mary Wilson, daughter of William Wilson. Born on 19 January 1836 at Armboth (by Thirlmere), William Wilson had been a farmer, but from 1875 was Manager or Proprietor of the Royal Oak Hotel, Keswick, and in 1883 took over at the Keswick Hotel, apparently as lessee from the Keswick Hotel Company. This led to J. Banks Wivell and Mrs Mary Wivell (nee Wilson) becoming involved with the Keswick Hotel, where in due time they became managers.

After 1918 their elder son, Alex Wivell, trained in catering and hotel matters in Switzerland and in 1931 became joint proprietor with his father of the Armathwaite Hall Hotel, Bassenthwaite Lake. The younger son, W. Dennis Wivell, also came out of the services. Having qualifications as an electrical engineer, he became established, by May 1919, as W. D. Wivell of Wivell's Coaches and Motors Ltd, of the Keswick Hotel Garage. This, in due course, brought W. D. Wivell into the Keswick Hotel proper. His father had already, back in 1912, figured as 'J. B. Wivell, proprietor' on the hotel notepaper, but this may have been a loose presentation of lessee, for in 1913 J. W. Pattinson, a CKPR Director, was on the Hotel Company Board and Peter Thompson, Secretary and General Manager of the Railway, was also interested. True proprietorship probably came a little later, but still in CKPR days, and the new partnership developed as J. & M. Wivell & Son (namely J. Banks Wivell and Mary, and WDW). This was a private family company, but one of the Pattinsons (JWP, presumably) was a Director, while the Chairman into these family days was Robert Jackson Holdsworth, of Bolton and Thornthwaite, who was on the CKPR Board from 1913 to 1923. W. D. Wivell and Mrs Wivell succeeded as proprietors and managers.

With the departure of Roedean School (who took their own bedding and equipment with them) at the end of 1945, the Wivells elected to sell their interest to Thomas Cooper Pattinson, of Windermere, who later vested all the shares in the Keswick Hotel Co Ltd, a Pattinson family company. Mr Shoesmith was appointed Manager and modernisation extended over several years, resulting in 58 bedrooms with private bathrooms, and other similar facilities. The Hotel Company was sold to J. Lyons & Company on 29 March 1972 – almost concurrent with the closure of the railway at Keswick – and they operated it as a 'Falcon Inn'. They resold it, in January 1978, to Trust House Forte (UK) Ltd, and further change of control has emerged in the 1990s.

The Keswick Hotel retains the external appearance that pleased the old CKPR Board in architects' drawings and on completion in the 1860s, and it retains an air of 'solid comfort' in keeping with its surroundings. To the student of railway history in general, and Keswick's railway history in particular, the former conservatory, with ante-room, beautiful stained glass screens, and entrance lobby from the main station platform, is particularly rewarding to view today.

This delightful stained glass screen is still well kept. The double doors are between the ante-room and lobby, leading from the Keswick Hotel and its conservatory to the station platform. The artists depicted in stained glass are Sir Peter Lely, Raphael Sanzio, Paul Veronese and Sir Godfrey Kneller. The picture was taken on 12 March 1985. *Harold D. Bowtell*

6. East of Keswick

A CKPR spectacular: by Briery Bobbin Mill and Greta Gorge

Milepost 13 (from Cockermouth Junction) was at Keswick station, MP14 at Briery platform and MP16½ on the approach to Threlkeld station. One may compare this section of the CKPR route with the Highland line in Killiecrankie Pass, between Perth and Inverness. But the Greta gorge section of the CKPR and its emergence, with suddenly wider views, at its eastern end had their own distinctive character. Trains travelled too quickly for the appreciation of two short tunnels and fully a dozen bridges – including eight spectacular bowstring girder under-line bridges by which the single-track railway crossed and recrossed the rocky river valley. (The various structures receive more detailed attention in the second volume.)

A platelayer's eye view, or that of the walker today, is, however, rewarding. At two points the new portions of the A66 road have broken in on the scene since 1972. On Keswick's outskirts, Brigham Forge, in the valley below (north of) the railway route, is eclipsed by the lofty skew road bridge. 'Big Tunnel' is beneath that bridge, and infilled, along with part of its approach cutting; the walker has to clamber up and over the road, or find access at Briery and walk back. There is also infilling east of bowstring bridge No 75 (Crozier Holme) where at MP16 the new road recrosses the route.

Climbing again, our old friend No 58396 is seen with the 11.50am Up train from Workington on 5 August 1950. The train is heading up the bank eastward out of Keswick. *E. S. Russell*

The scene in the Greta gorge as a 'Cauliflower' approaches with a Down passenger train; it would seem to have crossed bridge No 73 (Rowsome) and just crossed No 72, an under-line arch over Naddle Beck. *Richard L. Pattinson/CRA*

Briery bobbin mill and platform

Eastward of 'Big Tunnel', the railway barely squeezed along a rocky shelf between the river, with a massive retaining wall (below to the left) and the protective wall (above to the right). Just beyond this point a loop in the river provided the site for the bobbin mill and its cottages. In the 1820s waistcoats and similar woollens were manufactured here, then bobbin-making came in the 1830s, owners being in general the Coward family, but Coward, Philipson & Co Ltd from 1922 (although, strangely, a reference in 1867 is to Charles Christopherson). Import of timber was required, notably local hardwoods (sycamore, ash, beech and birch), but later teak from Burma and lancewood and boxwood from the Caribbean. Bobbins were despatched for the textile industries.

As early as 1867 the CKPR agreed in principle to provide a siding, but it was not until 1891 that a detailed layout and terms were agreed with Mr William Philipson and a siding for 20 wagons, with access (controlled by ground frame) facing Up trains, and a smaller internal loop siding were put in hand. Another internal siding diverged to run into the buildings. The bobbin trade was slack in

1902 and the charge for use of the siding was reduced from 1s to 6d per ton. In 1906 and 1911 further short extensions were made. In those days, bobbins were despatched by rail, bound for destinations that included St Petersburg in Russia. The mill closed in November 1958, at which time the siding layout was still in place, although used only for inwards coal in the preceding few years. A major sale at the premises took place on 3 June 1959 and the private siding agreement with the railway was formally terminated on 17 October of that year.

At a date that seems to have been soon after 1922, a wooden platform was constructed at Briery for use by workpeople arriving from Keswick (and also from Cockermouth) in the mornings and leaving at teatime, or lunchtime on Saturdays. This platform was placed on the Up side, with a wicket gate leading directly down into the mill yard. The condition of the wooden-faced platform deteriorated by the early 1930s. The LMS was 'watching the pennies' at this time of depression and slackness in industry, but the District Engineer had surplus pre-cast concrete units in stock, so it was rebuilt with these substantial facing units, and exists today. The daily calls for workmen, made by one train each way, are understood to have ceased wef Monday 17 November 1958, a week after cessation of production at the mill.

The site of the bobbin mill and some of its industrial buildings have been adapted and reconstructed tastefully to provide holiday accommodation; the workers' cottages, close

Proceeding east, after leaving 'Big Tunnel', a 'Tweedy' ground frame was unlocked by the key token to give access to the sidings at Briery bobbin mill. Stone-arched bridge No 63 carries the lane to the mill site and the platform is a little beyond. The ground frame at Flusco was of essentially the same design. *Richard L. Pattinson/CRA*

Briery bobbin mill platform, for workpeople, looking west. It was in daily use except on Sundays until 1958, when the mill closed. Its date of origin is obscure, but is probably soon after 1922, and its face was rebuilt, using precast concrete units, during the 1930s. *Richard L. Pattinson/CRA*

by the river bank, have become an attractive part of the scheme.

Approaching Threlkeld

The railway from Keswick next crossed the Glenderamackin, a tributary of the Greta, and reached Threlkeld station on the lower southern slopes of the broad valley that it was about to follow eastward. The station site was remote from the old Threlkeld village, seen three-quarters of a mile distant on the northern slopes of the valley, with the bulk of Blencathra (Saddleback) rising dramatically to its 2,847-foot summit about 1½ miles behind the village. The station was accessible from the by-road that heads south to St John's-in-the-Vale and Thirlmere. It also, opportunely, proved to be well-sited to serve major developments in quarrying and 'Threlkeld quarry village', which derived from these, in the later years of the 19th century.

Threlkeld station

Threlkeld station was originally on the single line, in the section from Keswick to Troutbeck (8¼ miles), and it was neither a crossing place nor a block post. A house for the station master was put in hand in 1865, on the Up side bank above the station, designed by architect Mr Ross and built by J. R. Harrison. A pair of railwaymen's cottages were also built, under plans of 1887, on the far side of the house and likewise facing west, at right angles to the line. By 1911 the near cottage was allocated to a signalman. All the houses are occupied today. By 1888 a modest waiting room, for quarry workers, was approved for construction on the platform, and in 1890 a shunting neck at the west end, on the Down side, was proposed.

In July 1892 the Railway's Engineer produced a plan for conversion of Threlkeld to a crossing station, with an island platform, a layout that contemplated early doubling over the 4¼ steeply-graded uphill miles east to Troutbeck. There was already a ground frame on the Up side, well to the east of the station layout. Also, some form of signalling applied in 1892, as on 1 July 1892 permissive block working was being operated from Threlkeld to Troutbeck for Up (ascending) trains and, wef 9 November 1892, Highgate signal box opened to break this section and absolute block working was introduced (for passengers) from Keswick (or Threlkeld) to Highgate and Troutbeck. It is not clear whether any electric tablet instrument working was introduced at Threlkeld at this time.

The engineer's plan of 1892 was soon adopted. The new platform was constructed on the Up side of the existing single running line, which thereafter became the Down line. A new Up line was laid round the other side of the platform, close in to the foot of the embankment on the northern boundary. The island platform created was the only one on the C&WR/CKPR route to take precisely this form of one Up and one Down face to a single island. The neat and workmanlike range of single-storey buildings erected on the platform included separate workmen's, gentlemen's and ladies' waiting rooms, with integral lavatories for the two latter rooms, together with a station office (with mullioned bay window to the platform and booking window to the booking hall). The hall was reached via a porch down at road level, a subway and ascending stairs. Architecturally, an unusual and attractive feature was the signal box, which formed part of the platform buildings at the western end; internal stairs ascended to an operating floor that was at about eaves level with the main range of buildings. The signal box was brought into use on 27 September 1893. On that day (or very close to it) Threlkeld became a crossing place, with electric tablet operation, and by 4 October 1893 the Board of Trade authorised the crossing of trains there.

Doubling from Threlkeld to Troutbeck was carried out between August 1893 and August 1894; the Board of Trade's provisional approval of the works followed in the latter month, with final approval in December. Double-line block working from Threlkeld to Highgate and Troutbeck was thus instituted. A small addition to the buildings shown in the accompanying photographs was the coalhouse-cum-lamproom (built in 1918) on the platform against the west wall of the signal box.

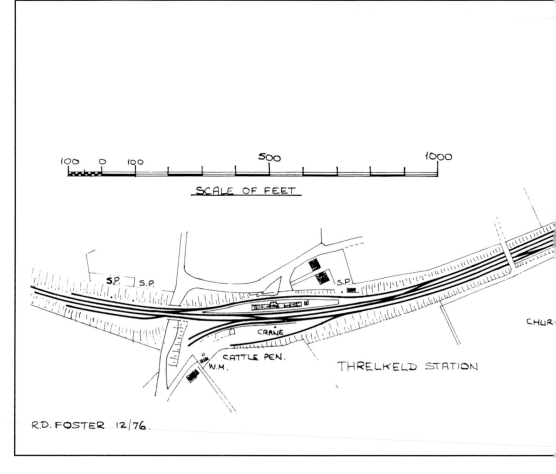

SCALE OF FEET

100   0   100   500   1000

S.P.   S.P.

S.P.

CRANE

CATTLE PEN.

W.M.

THRELKELD STATION

CHUR

R.D. FOSTER 12/76.

Above The layout at Threlkeld, essentially as created 1893-94 and modified down the years to the 1930s. *Drawn by Richard Foster*

Left This view is from the elevated signal box at Threlkeld at 12.28pm on 6 September 1948. No 28492 is arriving with the 10.23am Whitehaven-Penrith passenger train, and the fireman is preparing to surrender the token for the section from Keswick. *Harold D. Bowtell*

Right No 58389 is seen again on the 11.50am ex-Workington of 7 August 1950. This is the eastern end of Threlkeld station, with the signal box glimpsed and the corner of the station master's house (of 1865) above the bank on the right. *E. S. Russell*

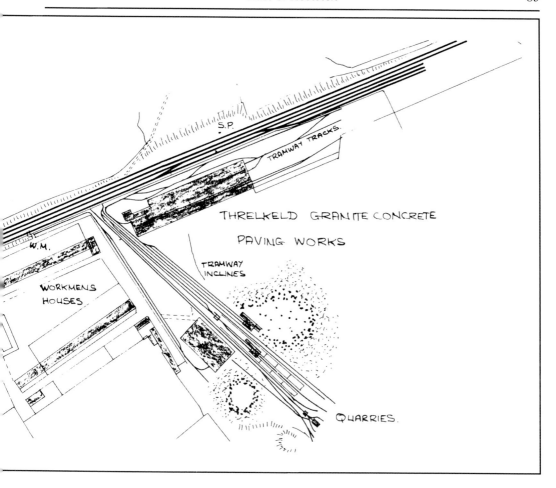

THRELKELD GRANITE CONCRETE PAVING WORKS

The Threlkeld station buildings of 1892-93, seen first from the west, showing the unusual integrated signal box (the lean-to shelter was a later addition), and in the second view from the east. Both pictures were taken in the 1960s. *Peter W. Robinson*

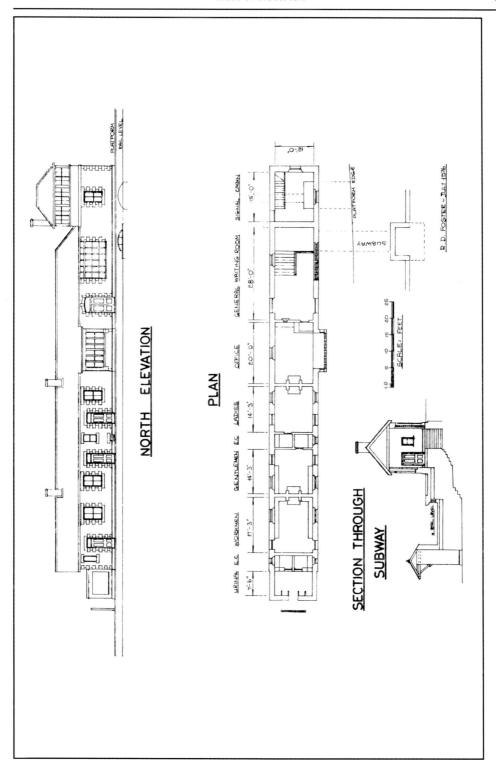

Elevations and plans of the Threlkeld station buildings, as reconstructed by LNWR historian Richard D. Foster.

This is the west end of Threlkeld's island platform, with the signal box glimpsed, shortly after reconstruction in 1892-93. Is the gentleman obscuring the locomotive bunker (second from right) the personable George Schollick, the long-serving first signalman here? The locomotive over towards the loading dock is an LNWR 0-6-2 'Coal Tank'. *Richard L. Pattinson/CRA*

The design of the entrance to Threlkeld station by its subway was, like the main buildings, tastefully executed. *Richard L. Pattinson/CRA*

From the point of view of passenger traffic, Threlkeld was a fairly typical wayside station, but visitors to Blencathra Sanatorium came here from its opening in 1904, and for many years there was a morning and evening train for quarry workers, from and to Keswick. Local goods traffic was on a small scale, with limited sidings on the south-west of the site. The most southerly had the odd cattle-pen on a small platform and could also handle coal, but there were never any coal cells. During circa 1890-94 Threlkeld was a railhead for the receipt of masonry, pipes and valves to be carted through the vale to Thirlmere for use in building Manchester Corporation's dam and aqueduct works. Like most CKPR stations, Threlkeld acquired acetylene gas lighting and the gas house was built on the bank, on the Up side, just east of the platform end.

The way to the quarry village and quarries was by the distinctly informal road past the porch entrance to the passenger station, thence close by the railway houses and soon turning over the spidery 'fly bridge' (No 81). The light construction of this bridge was restrictive, and in 1935 drawings were prepared for a new structure to cross the railway (two running lines and two siding lines at that point) diagonally, NW-SE, to the east of the 'fly bridge', to emerge opposite the lane that passed the west end of Railway Terrace (now Glenderamachin Terrace). This work was not done, and in about 1947 a roadway was made outside the southern boundary of the railway property, so that motor vehicles need not use the light bridge. Both routes remain.

From 4 December 1967 the double-track sections reverted to single-line working and the remaining signal boxes (including Threlkeld) closed. The station closed to goods wef 1 June 1964. It was unstaffed from 1 July

A 'Cauliflower' with an Up passenger is setting off from Threlkeld for some 5 miles of climbing at (mostly) 1 in 62, to the next stop at Troutbeck. The Down Home is a CKPR signal; the lamp top is open, the porter doubtless has his lamps out for cleaning and refilling with oil. Observe the arched lattice bridge of light construction, which at the time provided the only road access to the Quarry Company's premises. An independent lead from the station layout to the quarry sidings runs parallel (left). *Richard L. Pattinson/CRA*

A view eastward of Threlkeld station, looking back hazily to the lattice bridge shown in the previous picture. The three sidings for the granite quarry traffic are on the left with their loading bank left again. The Up Advance Starter is another CKPR signal. *Richard L. Pattinson/CRA*

1968, and passenger working ceased wef 6 March 1972, with closure of the line. The lever frame was taken out, but the attractive signal box and other buildings stood, vainly awaiting a saviour, until 1985; demolition took place during 1985-86, the 'gas house' also being razed in the spring of 1986.

Threlkeld quarries and their railway traffic
Back in 1874 the CKPR erected a shed at Threlkeld, partly for the use of the Saddleback Mining Company (John Jackson of Annan), which was carting lead ore from the other side of the valley for loading on rail; their successors brought traffic until circa the early 1920s.

There had for long been a small granite quarry in the hill immediately south-east of the station site, apparently a 'parish quarry' with a tradition that local people could work it at their pleasure. It was also a substantial source of stone for Boulton during construction of the CKPR in 1862-64. However, in 1877 it was taken over by Mr Bullen, of Barnard Castle, becoming known in time as Bottom Quarry, and the Railway Company undertook to lengthen the siding east of the station to accommodate, it is thought, 12 wagons. By 1883 the proprietors were the Cumberland Road Metal Company Ltd (Harkewitz & Bullen) who, while providing outward traffic, were not 'good payers'. A little later (1885-87) things were going their way and the quarry working was being expanded. In 1890-91 (by March) the huge retaining wall was built, with stone supplied free by the quarry owners, so that an extra 'back road' could be laid by the CKPR for quarry traffic – and in 1892-93 the third and final siding for this traffic was squeezed in, with lengthening eastward of these three

sidings following in 1898. The Granite Company built wagon shops at the end of these sidings, circa 1901-02. Plant was then developed for making macadam as well as paving flags. This was probably the peak period for these quarries, but they were still busy in 1921, when C. J. Allen reported that they provided the biggest part of the CKPR's freight. Trade declined in the 1920s, with much short-time working from 1926 (the General Strike) onwards and typically three day's work weekly.

The Company was reformed as the Threlkeld Granite Co Ltd in 1891. Mr Hermine Harkewitz was principal until his death (on 19 October 1904), but the controlling Board was widened to include businessmen with CKPR (and other) interests; Thomas Glasson and, later, J. W. Pattinson were Chairmen. Following association with the Cumberland Granite Co Ltd of Close quarries, Embleton, to form the Keswick Granite Co Ltd (incorporated 24 September 1936), quarrying operations were concentrated from 1936 to 1937 at Embleton,

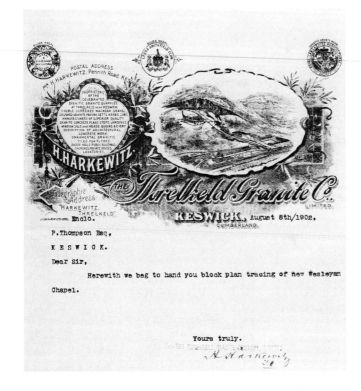

The setting, products and atmosphere of the Threlkeld Granite Co Ltd in Mr Harkewitz's day come though on this letterhead of 1902. Note the message. *Oswald Todhunter collection*

with a little site activity at Threlkeld itself in 1937-39, perhaps into 1940.

The Quarry Company ran a lorry morning and evening to convey its Threlkeld men to Close and home again. Emphasis was switched back from Embleton in 1948, but there was never major activity again, and one notes that the CKPR line ceased to be available after 1964. By 1973 employment was only about 50, with little actual quarrying. The last quarry working was in 1980-81, and complete closure followed in 1982.

Narrow gauge steam railway

The Threlkeld Granite Co Ltd developed a railway system of 2ft 4in gauge (approx). This brought stone out of Bottom Quarry, as it was exploited, but its exciting main line diverged in a southerly direction to reach Hill Top Quarry, about a mile from and above Hill Top Farm; this was the 'Spion Kop' quarry in the men's nomenclature, implying opening out in about 1900. There was a locomotive water tank at the trail-in from this quarry and in due course the narrow gauge line was extended, with sinuous curves as it followed the hillside well above the vale road to Thirlmere, until it reached Bramcrag Quarry; a lengthy face was developed and the main route of the railway here reached about 2½ miles. A little beyond the end of the line and down near the road, landmarks are 'The Bungalow', built in the 1890s by Manchester Corporation in connection with its Thirlmere project, and Bramcrag farmhouse. 'Klondyke' quarry (worked out well before the others) once had a branch line, north of 'Spion Kop'.

At the Threlkeld end of the route was a locomotive shed with two roads, complete with inspection pits and adjoining site workshops. Close by these buildings, stone was tipped into crushers and loaded by gravity to narrow gauge wagons, which descended self-acting rope-worked inclines (the drum side walls survive) to the tar plant and on to the buildings alongside the standard gauge

Out on the narrow gauge to southward, above St John's-in-the-Vale, was Bramcrag Quarry, where *George* V, an 0-4-0 well tank engine built by Andrew Barclay in 1921, is seen drawing out a load destined for Threlkeld incline top, the crusher and processing, and despatch by the CKPR line. *John Jameson*

Above the narrow gauge incline, the locomotive shed had two roads. The shed housed the three small steam locomotives to work the traffic from the quarries, which were away up behind the camera and were formerly reached by the private line. Threlkeld (old) village is largely in view across the valley, on 27 June 1984. *Harold D. Bowtell*

sidings and adjacent loading bank, where the paving slabs were made. By 1923 the narrow gauge line continued right along the bank beside the sidings. Three locomotives are known, and all survived until around 1939, latterly in the shed:

Threlkeld: An 0-4-0ST with 8in x 12in outside cylinders, built by W. G. Bagnall, Works No 1608 of May 1900.
Edward VII: An 0-4-0ST with 8in x 12in outside cylinders, built by W. G. Bagnall, Works No 1685 of April 1902.
George V: An 0-4-0WT, with 7in x 11in outside cylinders, built by Andrew Barclay, Works No 1734 of 1921.

All came new to the Company and the dates reconcile with the Boer War period, also with the further development at Bramcrag after the 1914-18 wartime slackening of quarry trade. Usually one locomotive was 'spare' while two worked, their trains crossing at the intermediate loop near 'Spion Kop'. Each trip would bring down 16 or 17 30cwt-capacity loaded trucks; between them the two working engines made up to 10 journeys per day. Quarry workers were at one time brought down on the narrow gauge 'mail' train at the end of the working day, and this naming extended to the CKPR/LMS workers' train, stabled in its short siding at Threlkeld during the day. This was the 'Boer Train', used also by Mr Bragg, the manager, and his sons and office staff. In 1932 a set of LNWR coaches was observed with an endboard inscribed

'KESWICK & THRELKELD WORKMAN'S TRAIN'.

Threlkeld quarry village: a lively community

The commercial development of the granite quarries has been dated from 1877, with subsequent progressive expansion from 1885 to 1902, and intermittent busy periods until 1925. 'Commuters' were brought by the train from Keswick, but the quarry owners encouraged immigration from other parts of the country, including Leicestershire, known for its granite quarries. In Top Row (nowadays known as Blencathra View) 12 'tin' houses and six narrow stone houses were built, probably all in the 1890s. In 1890 Bottom Row was under construction, starting from its eastern end with the Company office, then six particularly dignified houses. The whole terrace was seemingly not completed through to its western end until the late 1890s. Its official title was Railway Terrace, now Glenderamachin Terrace, with no view of the railway below but a fine vista of the river valley and awe-inspiring Blencathra. It was the reported overcrowding of the quarry village, in January 1887, that led the CKPR to build the two cottages near the station for its own staff. At its peak, probably in the early 20th century, the Granite Company is said to have employed around 200 men, including local residents and daily comers.

About 100 children attended the quarry village school, located on the top edge of the village. It was a delightful site and the Railway

During the early 20th century heyday of Threlkeld quarries, this is the vista from the top of the narrow gauge incline that conveyed trucks of crushed granite to the loading bank alongside the standard gauge sidings shown on page 93. The CKPR line crosses just beyond the foot of the site at right angles. To the left are the horse-keeper's house (white), the bothy or lodging house (in dark 'tin'), the reading room (white, gabled), the end gable of the terrace of 'tin' houses in Top Row, the Company office (above the tarmac plant), and the gables of the tall, permanent houses of Railway Terrace (now Glenderamachin Terrace). *John Jameson*

Company contributed £25 to the cost of the building in 1897 – and this helped to stave off the appointment of a school board, which would levy a compulsory rate. Similar thoughts and altruism merged to produce a voluntary subscription of £5 per annum to the Vicar of Threlkeld in support of the Church of England school in the old village across the valley. It dates from 1849, when it replaced an earlier school, and is still active today. The quarry school prospered for many years, but by 1951 was down to 11 children and it closed in July of that year.

At the eastern end of the top street was a reading room, and behind it the 'bothy' or lodging house (a 'tin' building), no doubt provided for new arrivals and single men. Above this again was the horse-keeper's house and, topmost, the stables; these last have been reconstructed to become a house. The Wesleyan chapel, opened on 14 October 1903

and converted circa 1981 to a handsome residence, accompanied by cricket and football grounds, with one-time pavilion, rounded off the facilities. Typically, in the 12 months from August 1901 to July 1902 railway excursion bookings from Penrith brought the Working Men's Football Club, and its supporters, on three Saturdays. On 19 July 1902 the Edenhall Cricket Club and its friends had similar facilities to Threlkeld.

Although the public buildings have all ceased to perform their intended functions, this remains a significant village, although not all householders are all-year residents nowadays; some of the cottages are 'holiday homes'.

Threlkeld railway folk

An early station master was John Smith, then soon Gresley Wolton took over in September 1866; that was still at the wayside station with no crossing facility and no industry, and the pay was 18 shillings weekly. A uniform was also provided, together with a house and an additional 2 shillings weekly from August 1872. The personable signalman on the opening of the new box of 1893 and throughout the other major developments of that period was George Schollick. His diary, with entries through to 1927, is of much local interest.

In due time the quarry business accounted for the employment of a station clerk (Joe Ridley by the 1920s-1930s) and a yardsman; this, in 1913, was W. Notman, who joined the army and sadly was killed, as a Sergeant, in 1916. Signalmen of later days included Joseph Farrer (son of the station master) and Edwin K. Nelson, of Tebay, the latter in 1934-36 – he had previously had a year at Penruddock – and Bob Wren from circa 1961 until closure of the box on 3 December 1967. He died in October 1984, a loss to many friends. The elder Joseph Farrer, then Fred Johnston, were station masters here, until Mr Johnston's death in 1936. Cecil Oldfield came from a career on the Furness Railway and FR section of the LMS from 1912 to 1937, to be station master from circa 1937 to 1945, later going on Preston way.

Eastward to Highgate and Troutbeck
Most of the 4¾ miles from Threlkeld to Troutbeck climbed at 1 in 62, and the summit of the line (889 feet) was about half a mile beyond Troutbeck station. (This section receives further mention in the second volume.) From MP16½ at Threlkeld, the way today is clear to walk to nearing MP18 (Guardhouse under-line bridge). At over-line bridge No 87 is the early pair of CKPR cottages known as Moor Cottages, later Hill Cottages, and now Hill Cottage. The house nearest the bridge was occupied by Jack Greenhow, a well-known length ganger in the early 20th century, his elder son being William Greenhow, who became senior carter at Keswick. Lower down, in the Wallthwaite community, there had been a public house, thought to be in demand during the railway widening of the 1890s. Up the hill above the cottages, the present handsome 'Birkett Hill'

was known as 'Old Hill House' and earlier 'Old Hill Hog House' and 'Gin Hog'.

The Mosedale viaduct, between Hill Cottage and Highgate, was the longest of the route's many bridges. It is still impressive seen in evening light from the A66 road, about three-quarters of a mile distant, but can better be viewed by following the valley of the Mosedale beck on foot, upstream from Wallthwaite. Highgate is reached by over-line bridge No 91, which commands a view of the site of the children's platforms of 1908-28 and the CKPR houses of 1898, with a glimpse of the little block signal box of 1892-1931 (eastward). Gillhead viaduct is close to the A66 road, nearing Troutbeck station.

Troutbeck station
The station was immediately east of MP21 and over-line bridge No 97, which carried the road (A5091) to Matterdale and Ullswater. This bridge, like others, was remodelled for the doubling of 1893-94, but was demolished in 1984, the road now crossing the former trackbed on the level. Passengers would come from Mungrisdale and Mosedale hamlets in the north and Matterdale to the south, together with those from scattered farmhouses and perhaps, hopefully, tourists and climbers bound for Patterdale at the head of Ullswater.

In 1862 a station site near Wallthwaite was considered and 'Hutton Moor' was mentioned in this connection, so the site of Moor Cottages may have been in mind – but it was decided, in June 1862, to build the station 'at the Troutbeck road'. Thus Troutbeck station was an original facility of 1865. It had one platform, with buildings, on the north side of the single line. A Down loop with a second platform and signal box were added in 1874. The doubling eastward, to Penruddock, was carried out in 1900-01. The Up platform building provided a station office, general waiting room and ladies' waiting room. A house for the station master was rented at the start, but by 1869 a two-storey house was being built and, as can be seen, abutted directly on to the back of the single-storey platform building.

The Down platform of 1874 carried a timber waiting shed, which had a long life. It

Mosedale viaduct, the longest bridge on the CKPR . 'Cauliflower' No 28589 is working the 2.10pm Workington-Penrith on 7 August 1950, with its maximum permitted load of five carriages. The gradient here climbed at almost 1 in 62. The dark slopes of Blencathra are across to the right. *E. S. Russell*

A classic scene on the western approach to Troutbeck station in BR days. Ivatt '2MT' 2-6-0 No 46491 is heading east on Saturday 31 July 1965 with a train from Keswick to Manchester and Crewe, comprised of BR and LMS rolling-stock. The train is running 'wrong road' following the temporary introduction of single-track working over the former Down line on this section in the spring of 1965. Once again, Blencathra ('Saddleback') dominates the horizon. *Derek Cross*

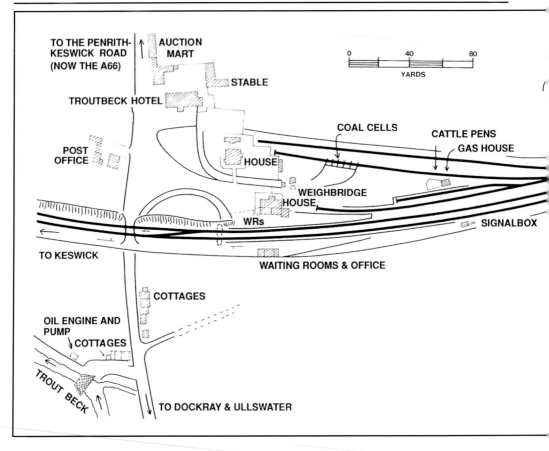

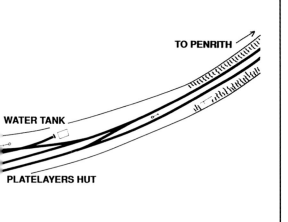

Above Troutbeck station track layout.

Left Troutbeck station, looking eastward from bridge No 97 (Matterdale Road – A5091) on 9 October 1966, when it was but little changed. *Harold D. Bowtell*

became the practice from the days of Joe Cutts as station master to hold Sunday afternoon services and a Sunday school in the Up-side premises, and later in the room on the Down side. Furniture included a harmonium, which remained even after the station closed.

The small yard, with its eastward trailing connection on the Up side, was little expanded from its 1865 form. It had two short sidings close to the Up running line and was served by the loading bank, crane, cattle pens (the first of which dated from 1872) and a small goods shed. There was an original long siding with coal drops at its remote end and another long siding inserted behind it. John Stubbs was the coal merchant, then Mr Cutts (station master) took over. Timber from Ullswater estates was hauled over on long horse-drawn wagons at one time. The outer siding and the coal drops were taken out in 1955, the beginnings of terminal decline; in 1966 one short siding remained. The acetylene gas house was beside the cattle pens. Troutbeck's award-winning station gardens must not be overlooked in this history.

Also on the Up side, near the convergence of the yard tracks, was a locomotive water tank, but in 1914 the tank was reported to be empty and the pump engine was replaced that year by a new oil engine. Locomotive water was still available in later years, by gravity supply, with supplementary pumping from the stream when necessary. In 1955 there was a plan to convert the tank house to a tool store.

Troutbeck's autumn sheep sales were held at the mart adjoining the nearby Troutbeck

Right Also in October 1966, a westward view from the east end of the station, showing that the yard had been curtailed to one siding. The signal box, built by Saxby & Farmer in 1874, was in the first group of proper lever frames and cabins installed on the CKPR. The latter-day lever frame from Troutbeck box was removed (1984-85) by the Derwent Railway Society, for the National Railway Museum. *Harold D. Bowtell*

Hotel, producing traffic for the railway over many years. An early industrial connection was a siding of circa 1867 to 'the tileworks adjoining the station'. This would be Mr Miller's brickyard, where, in May 1868, his men caused accidental damage to an engine and a wagon belonging to the LNWR. The brick and tile works was on land behind the Down platform and its siding ran to stops near the Matterdale road embankment, with rail access by a trailback behind the signal box. It seems to have finished by 1914; the private siding was removed in 1915 and the Down platform was extended eastward.

The exploitation of minerals brought traffic to Troutbeck yard for despatch. Lead mined by the Greenside Mining Company (Ltd) was a long-standing if intermittent traffic. The mines were 1½ to 2 miles west of Glenridding (Ullswater), up into the mountain valley and the slopes of Helvellyn. The office was at Greenside, Glenridding, and the engineer-manager resided (certainly, from 1912) at 'Greenside Lodge'. He was for long W. H. Borlase, who wrote a paper on the mines in the mid-1890s and reported frequently until at least 1928 to J. W. Pattinson, the miller, of Whitehaven. He was principal of the Mining Company and a CKPR Board member from 1903 to 1923.

Mining dated from the first quarter of the 19th century and in 1867 the Company signed a 10-year agreement with the CKPR for traffic via Troutbeck station. Rates were quoted for consignment of their products to Liverpool, Skipton, Chester and Glasgow. They were then described as lead manufacturers with mine, works (namely smelting) and also 'lodging shops' at the mine for workers. There were problems circa 1867-70, as not all consignments were handled by way of the CKPR, as contracted. In October 1877 they proposed carting part of their traffic to Penrith and the agreement lapsed, but the earlier arrangements were resumed in 1879.

Hydro-electric generation powered an overhead-wire electric locomotive from circa 1892. In 1910 the mines were in a poor way, but Mr Borlase was an incurable optimist and saw prospects in the discovery, on 24 October 1910, of a fresh lode of lead. In February 1911

new plant was brought over from Troutbeck station, and the use of a steam traction wagon was commonplace, notwithstanding the County Council having forbidden this traffic to cross Dockray Bridge on the route! On one occasion in April 1912 the 'traction' made the entire journey, Greenside Mines-Troutbeck-Whitehaven, in the day, and was expected to spend the next day returning. Bob Hope and Geordie Craig are remembered on the steam lorry. The mines prospered during the First World War and in December 1915 the War Office released men to work there. Smelting is understood to have ceased in 1919, with the lead subsequently sent to Troutbeck for consignment by rail to Newcastle-upon-Tyne for smelting. The Greenside traffic via Troutbeck station did not end until the late 1930s.

The Penrith & District Road Carrying Company, a subsidiary of the Glenridding Lead Mining Company, had acquired a 'steam waggon', Sentinel No 5676 of 1924, with registration EC 5927. It was regularly employed conveying lead ore and chippings from the Greenside mine to Troutbeck station. On 2 June 1932, driven by two Glenridding men, it was carrying 6 tons of 'chippings' when, on a downhill part of the run, the steering is understood to have failed; the men jumped clear as the waggon ran off the road into a ravine. There it lay until circa 1954-55, when some form of dam-burst caused a severe flood and the lorry's remains were swept to a lower level. Removable parts including the steam engine were removed for scrap. Then, in June 1988, Richard Straughan, of Appleby, surveyed the scene, obtained the Lead Company's permission and secured a crane and the help of two men, including Eddie Poole, son of the 1932 driver. The vehicle was lifted out, including the boiler, with the Sentinel maker's plate still on the cabside. The water tank was recovered from a place further downstream in August 1988. The chassis was exhibited at the Cumbria Show in 1989. Mr Straughan restored the 'waggon' to running order and by August 1992 it was a 'runner' at the Summerlee Heritage Trust's notable and developing site, at Coatbridge.

Carrock Mines, near Mungrisdale, were also using Troutbeck station in the 1930s. Their initial prospectus, of June 1904, had written up the prospects in glowing terms, under the title of The Carrock Mines Ltd, with directors J. Wright Wilson, 'iron merchant' of Penrith, another director from Leicester and two from the City of London; the plan was to lease 5,000 acres of Carrock Fell properties, roughly 5 miles from the station.

An obscure reference by the Permanent Way Committee in CKPR records dated 4 November 1885 proposed to remove the east end of the quarry siding further from the main line; this was quoted as 'west of Troutbeck station', and the Cumberland Road Metal Company was mentioned. The implication is of a siding in section at that time.

The diary of George Schollick (of Threlkeld) recorded that on 10 September 1913 a horse and cart ran away from the station at Troutbeck and headed towards Threlkeld. It ran into the waggonette from the Lake Hotel, Keswick. One horse was killed and two passengers seriously hurt.

The first station master at Troutbeck was William Richardson, at 19 shillings weekly with uniform and house provided, typical terms for 1865. In August 1868 he was relieved on account of what was described as 'irregularities'. His successor, John Smith, was appointed in September 1868, on the same terms, rising to 21 shillings per week in August 1872 and 23 shillings in November 1874. However, in that month he 'absconded', leaving the accounts practically straight. Station master Walton retired in November 1912 on account of old age after giving 'long and faithful service'. He was awarded a gratuity of £30. He was followed in November 1912 by J. M. Cutts, hitherto Foreman Porter at Keswick, and he was in charge at Troutbeck until about 1926. Thompson Simpson would be the last station master from circa 1926 until 1932, after which Troutbeck was placed under the command of Threlkeld's station master.

Almost traditionally, there was a Watson at Troutbeck: Joseph Watson was for long the signalman, until his retirement in 1946, while his son, Edward Watson (still resident in the district at the time of writing) spent most of his career on the station. In 1913 Richard Hebson was the senior signalman, and had been at Troutbeck a good many years, with Joseph Watson as 'relief signalman' at that

Troutbeck's Up Advance Starting signal, a CKPR signal with a flat cap, is seen at the top of the bank, looking east through 'Summit bridge'. This occupation bridge was rebuilt for the track doubling with four main steel girders and concrete jack arches between them – indicative of changing civil engineering practices around the turn of the century. *Richard L. Pattinson/CRA*

time. It is thought that the term 'relief' was used by the CKPR to indicate a porter-signalman. Nathan Routledge had shared the signal box circa 1901-13 and tragically J. Whitham, relief signalman, was killed by an engine on 12 January 1906.

The Company's rule in 1907 was that the senior signalman at these smaller stations performed 11 hours duty daily, and for the remainder of the working day the box was operated by the porter-signalman, who also had hours allocated on the platform to make up a full day of 11-12 hours. In its later years Troutbeck box was not manned constantly; a porter-signalman was in the box as required by traffic. The pair of houses opposite the station (one now the post office) was owned by the Railway. Signalman Dick Hebson and Joe Watson were long-time residents, with their families.

Goods traffic ceased at Troutbeck wef 1 June 1964, and the signal box closed wef 21 November (or 5 December) 1966. It had a closing switch, so communication could be connected through from Threlkeld to Penruddock. Single-line working, from Keswick to Penrith No 1 box, applied from 4 December 1967, on a 'one engine in steam' basis. The station was unstaffed from 1 July 1968, and final closure (for passengers) was wef 6 March 1972.

Penruddock station

This was another wayside station, 2¼ miles eastward of Troutbeck, with a few houses nearby and the tiny villages at Motherby and Penruddock each about a half a mile distant. Originally in 1865 (or very shortly afterwards) it was a crossing place on the single line. The loop was lengthened 30 yards westwards in 1870, with a siding beyond, and in 1873 this siding was taken into the loop, in order to allow the longest mineral trains to cross. Signalling was concentrated in a box in 1874, electric tablet working (and exchange of tablets) came circa 1891, and double-line block working to Troutbeck in 1901, but the line was never doubled between Penruddock and Blencow.

Unlike other stations on the CKPR, Penruddock had staggered platforms. The

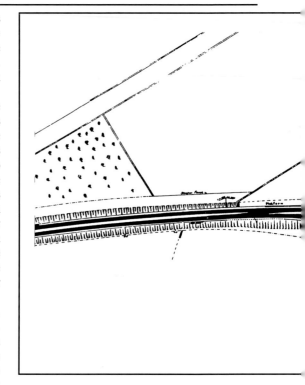

signal box (as rebuilt circa 1896) prudently overlooked the midway barrow crossing between the east end of the Up platform and the west end of the Down. The neat stone building on the Up side was closely comparable with that at Troutbeck, but had a slightly hipped roof at its eastern end. Again, a small wooden building graced the Down platform. A house for the station master was purchased from Mrs Sarah Bailey, widow, in good time (July 1863) for the opening in 1865. This was presumably the house on the roadside near the Up-side approach, occupied by station masters and provided with a path leading directly to the station approach.

The goods yard, on the Up side, effectively provided a short trailing siding behind the box, a short back siding eastward with a platform, and a longer siding eastward serving a cattle pen on the platform, a coal landing and three coal cells. A 3-ton-capacity crane was in the original equipment. At the west end of the Down platform, a 'horse and carriage landing' (later also available for motor car vans) was installed in 1882, trailing

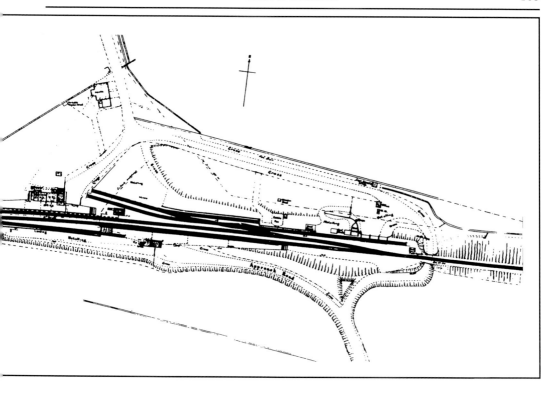

Penruddock station is reproduced here from an LMS plan. The horse dock, south of the running lines, and the coal cells, north and extreme right, receive mention in the story of Penruddock. The station master's house, well to the north of the station, still stands today.

'Cauliflower' No 28589, working the 10.20am from Penrith, is leaving Penruddock station westward, under bridge No 103 (A591), with Motherby and Greystoke to the left, on 7 August 1950. *E. S. Russell*

An eastward view at Penruddock, showing the staggered platforms, the CKPR-designed signal box and two CKPR signals nearest the camera. The dock for horse boxes and other like traffic is on the Down side (right) and beyond the coal cells (far left) the line crosses Penruddock viaduct. *Richard L. Pattinson/CRA*

off the down line and accompanied by a convenient crossover. This facility met the needs of the Howards (Henry Howard was a member of the CKPR Board from 1876 to 1914) of Greystoke Castle and their guests. Before the First World War horses were unloaded some half-dozen times each year, for hunting. In the years just before 1914 'Yoemanry' of the Northumberland Fusiliers came by way of Penruddock, with their horses, bound for summer camp held in fields beside the road between Motherby and Greystoke. Timber from the Greystoke estate (for pit-props) was loaded, in 1919, while in the war years from 1939 to 1945 this horse landing was again used for loading timber. Special cattle for export were also loaded similarly. The short Up side (east) siding was taken out in 1940 and the crossover was removed circa 1965. The station had the usual gas house and lighting.

The coal depot has been mentioned and it particularly served Greystoke and its surrounding area. Following the pattern found commonly on the NER, the Penruddock

station master enjoyed coal rights, although not exclusively; the coal merchant who operated from Penruddock depot thus found himself in competition with the station master! The merchant until 1921 was Mr Thompson, who retired that autumn in his 80s, and on 21 October 1921 Mr John Mandale, of Greystoke, took over, shortly after coming out of the army. He rented two coal cells – commonly styled 'coal vaults' in CKPR parlance – for use with bottom-door wagons and for storage, but also used the 'coal landing' for the discharge of side-door wagons. In his earlier days his coal came chiefly from Whitehaven (in bottom-door wagons) and from the Allerdale Coal Company's Buckhill Colliery (on the C&WJnR's Northern Extension line). Later, coal came from Wharncliffe in Yorkshire (and Hickleton Main) and a very good quality coal from Easington in Durham – and this was ordered in side-door wagons to minimise breakage during discharge. Local delivery was achieved for many years using traditional horse-drawn four-wheeled coal carts. However, from the

1930-35 period, Mr Mandale bagged his coal and delivered it in a Ford 1-ton motor lorry. His railway wagons were shunted off the local goods trains into the siding behind the box, and from there he pushed them to his depot in the east end of the long siding.

From 29 shillings per ton in the early 1920s, the price of coal delivered at Penruddock station fell during the ensuing years to 23s 6d per ton. Profit to the merchant was around 1d per hundredweight. The working day began at 7.30am. On Tuesdays John Mandale (a cheerful 90 years of age at the time of writing) would lend a hand to push loaded cattle wagons through to the siding behind the box, so that they could be picked up by the engine of the 8.15am (and thereabouts) passenger train, en route to Penrith, for the weekly auction mart. Mr Keith Mandale, son of John, took over eventually and has run the coal business from Penrith, and now Blencow, station yards.

Penruddock's first station master was William Reay, at 21 shillings weekly with uniform and house; he was transferred in January 1872 to Bassenthwaite Lake, a promotion in status if not in pay, and later held the premier position of station master at Keswick. John Tinnion came from being station master at Blencow in January 1872 (a promotion) and tendered his resignation in October 1906, the board responding with a gift of £25, in view of 'very long and faithful service'. John Blackburn, promoted from station master at Embleton, came in October 1906, at a salary of 25 shillings per week, but was appointed to Bassenthwaite Lake in August 1908, when Joseph Todhunter (formerly station master at Braithwaite) was appointed. He served until September 1921, when he moved to Bassenthwaite Lake. John Clapham, previously parcels clerk at Keswick, was appointed in his stead, at £200 per annum, plus 5%, and he was thus John Mandale's competitor for coal sales, and stayed to be the last station master at Penruddock, which was placed initially under Troutbeck, then, from 1932, Blencow. He lived in the house, which was afterwards occupied by other railwaymen. The first porter at Penruddock was Thomas White (appointed July 1864) at 12 shillings per week and, it is interesting to note, with house. Mr T. Thompson followed him in 1873; maybe it was he who took on the coal merchant's business.

In the years before 1914 William Ridley was the senior signalman, and likewise, in 1919, his son, Syd Ridley, joined the CKPR here as junior porter. Mr J. Todhunter (then living at Motherby) was the 'relief signalman' based here; he was 'fined' in December 1909 for 'irregularity in working the train tablet'. This was a serious offence, for only by rigorous operation of the tablet system could safety be maintained on a single-line railway. Later Syd Ridley (1905-1983), a stalwart character who long outlived the CKPR and even the local line itself, became signalman here (his father having died as signalman on 8 April 1927) with George Watson (Jnr) coming as his colleague, from local permanent way work, in which he had followed his father. They are not to be confused with other well-known local Watsons, whose service was principally at Troutbeck.

Closure of the signal box came with the changes of 4 December 1967. The station had closed to goods wef 1 June 1964, became unstaffed from 1 July 1968, and finally closed (with the line) wef 6 March 1972.

East from Penruddock

Departing eastward from Penruddock, a signal post on the Down side carried LNWR-type corrugated steel arms for the Up Starting signal and the Down Home signal; this arrangement lasted until the end of signalling on the line and probably dated from the remodelling of circa 1896. Separate signals had been in use a few years earlier, but the steel arms are likely to have replaced CKPR items in LMS days. The Penruddock viaduct (bridge No 105) was reduced from nine arches to four by infilling in 1920, but still stands today, unlike the ensuing under-line bridge No 106, demolished 1982-83.

Penruddock station (MP23½) to Blencow station (MP27½ approximately) was always single track, mostly descending eastward, concluding on a downgrade of 1 in 70. Between MP25, at Kirkbarrow Wood, and

Stanier 2-6-4T No 42594 represents the large tank locomotives permitted on the route from 1939, and indeed a little earlier, as they did not require the larger turntable. This is the 'Lakes Express' to London on 22 July 1960. Penruddock viaduct, which had nine arches (subsequently reduced by infilling), survives today, but under-line bridge No 106, beneath the engine, was demolished in 1982. *Derek Cross*

MP27, at Bunkers Wood, nearing Blencow, the route describes a bold sweep north, then east again, in order to negotiate the contours. On the south-north portion, after bridge No 111 (Green Lane, over-line) are two limeworks sites, and a notable cutting.

Harrison's limeworks siding, Flusco

Mr Joseph Harrison proposed opening out a limestone quarry around 1907, and by 1912 his limeworks was established. However, it was not until 1916 that his Flusco siding was commissioned, south of under-line bridge 113 (Flusco bridge) and precisely at MP26. The turn-out faced Down trains and the ground frame was released by the Blencow-Penruddock tablet. The title became Harrison's Lime Works Ltd, and the works embraced quarrying, crushing and processing, and included kilns. Traffic increased and even kept the line open for a time after closure of the Penrith-Keswick branch line on 6 March 1972. 'One engine' working applied from Penrith No 1 box to Flusco Siding until closure wef 19 June 1972. The site changed hands latterly and was closed by Amalgamated Roadstone Corporation circa 1980.

In 1923 there were a couple of internal standard gauge sidings, incorporating twin loops, on banking above the CKPR running line, and by 1954 several roads were noted; there was a cable drum for standard gauge haulage. The quarry (hidden from the CKPR line) employed a 2-foot-gauge internal system. In 1924 a network of hand-operated tracks are recalled on the quarry floor, with a steam-powered cable incline at one end for haulage up to the crusher. At that time a single steam locomotive, kept clean but not in use, stood on an isolated track in the quarry bottom. It has been reputed that a steam 0-4-0T (by German builders Orenstein & Koppel) named *Fleetwood* was eventually buried at this site. A tentative identity, from recent research, is O&K No 5131 of 6 February 1912, supplied originally to Caffin & Company. The narrow gauge layout in 1954 included a steam winder by Clarke Chapman, an incline, and two four-wheeled internal combustion locomotives, one being in a dismantled state.

Flusco quarry siding

This siding connection was just north of bridge No 113, on the Down side of the single line and with entry facing Down trains, with a ground frame released by the token. It was of earlier date than Harrison's limeworks siding, and served 'Flusco Ballast Quarry' (the older spelling Fluskew being used at first). This was seemingly purchased circa 1890 by the CKPR for its own use, and there was one standard gauge siding alongside the running line. In November 1890 the CKPR proposed to purchase a stonebreaker and engine for the quarry. A tramway bogie accident on 15 September 1910 implies the existence of an internal narrow gauge layout. The index entry for a CKPR plan (undated) was titled 'Flusco Engine Shed', and this may hint at a locomotive. The use of the ballast quarry declined – in 1918 the CKPR was trying to sell the engine and crusher – and it was closed about 1922. In the working timetable of 3 October 1921 a call was still shown, and in 1921-22 a trip was made about one day weekly to remove material by rail.

St Andrews cutting

North of the old ballast quarry siding, the line, on a right-hand curve, passed through a rock cutting, itself topped by Low Fluskew Woods and hemmed in at its midpoint by St Andrews over-line bridge (No 115), which featured a stone arch on rock abutments. This was a

blind spot for locomotive drivers and in the exceptional snows of early 1940 it also became a snow block. The tragedy that occurred on that occasion is described in the second volume. Round the curve, and through the next over-line bridge, the bracketed Home signals and station of Blencow came into view.

Blencow station

This station was west of under-line bridge No 117. Here the railway crossed the by-road from the villages of Little and Great Blencow (up to 2 miles north) and the Clickham Inn crossroads on the former A594 (now the B5288). This road continues south through Newbiggin village (a mile south of the station) to reach the former B5288 (now merged into the A66). The station was named Newbiggin when planned, but by May 1864 the alternative names favoured were Greystoke (2 miles to the west) and Dacre (3 miles to the south). At the opening, in January 1865, Blencowe was adopted, but by July 1865 Bradshaw was listing Blencow (with no final 'e'), although the archaic form was commonly used by the Railway Company for a few more years. The station was on a single line, with the sole platform and buildings on

This view of the approach to Blencow station, looking east, is included to show the 'Cauliflower' turning sharply right from the Down platform road into the access line for Blencowe Limeworks, installed in 1936. Its train is seemingly standing in the Up loop (left). There is an LNWR Down Starting signal (on the right), but the Up Starter is of CKPR origin. *Richard L. Pattinson/CRA*

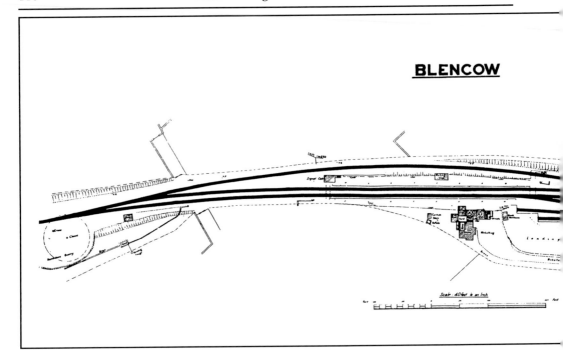

Above Blencow station, as recorded on an LMS plan, but drawn before the Blencowe Limeworks link of 1936 was installed; this curved off to the south.

Above This 7 August 1950 scene (from the east end of the Down platform) shows the Blencowe Limeworks access line cutting away right, across the tracks of the small yard, round the end of the cattle dock and across the carriageway approach to the station, heading for the works. No 45230, a Stanier 'Black 5' 4-6-0, is climbing briskly with the Down 'Lakes Express', comprised of four corridor coaches in red and cream livery, strengthened by two non-corridors, probably from Penrith, in LMS/BR darker red. *E. S. Russell*

Right Lime traffic is prominent in this Keswick-Carlisle goods, seen at Blencow on 3 August 1963, hauled by Ivatt Class '2MT' 'Mogul' No 46455. The train is taking the Up goods loop behind the platform. *D. F. Tee*

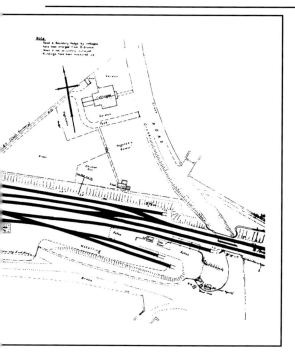

architect Mr Ross and built by J. R. Harrison, whose tender was accepted in March 1865; a substantial two-storey house resulted, behind the station premises and almost contiguous with them. Much later the acetylene gas house (for lighting) was built, abutting on the west elevation of the platform buildings. A carbide store was a separate structure, a short distance away. There were modest sidings on the Down side and, after the dramatic runaway of 26 December 1889, a shunting neck eastward was authorised.

Blencow was not provided with a crossing loop before the line eastward to Redhills Junction, 2 miles, was doubled; this was done between March 1900 and June 1901, the opening being on Sunday 2 June 1901. Up and Down running roads were then made through the station, converging to a single line to the west, and an Up platform was provided, with a one-room timber waiting shed. There are indications that the additional track created through the station was the Down line, in which case the original platform face was cut back. The signal box was built at the Down (west) end of the new platform and Blencow thus became a block post, with a single track (with electric token) westward and a double-line block eastward. A long siding was

the Down (southern) side. The single-storey building included an office and two waiting rooms but, unlike Troutbeck and Penruddock, two gables faced the platform.

The station master's house was designed by

installed at this time, entered in the facing direction by Up trains and passing behind the new Up platform to converge short of the under-line roadway. This provided a useful Up goods loop, allowing a lime train from Flusco, or other goods, to be held while passenger workings were handled at the station. Coal was accommodated with three cells on the Down side siding, which trailed back to near the under-line bridge.

An important development of the mid-1930s was the coming of the Blencowe (note spelling) Lime Co Ltd, south of the station, established by Mr John Farrer. A peculiar lead was completed for traffic in November 1936, leaving the yard access line after its divergence from the Down running line and taking a sweeping curve that cut across the cattle siding and likewise crossed the station roadway, in order to reach the limeworks. Substantial traffic from the works was developed between 1936 and 1939, and also during the war years, notably to Lanarkshire Steel and Colville's Dalzell Steelworks at Motherwell and Clyde Iron Works, as well as Glengarnock Works on the Glasgow & South Western line. In 1954 there was still an extensive internal 2-foot-gauge layout in the works area, serving crushing plant and kilns. There were many 2-foot-gauge wagons and two internal-combustion locomotives, respectively by Hudson-Hunslet, Works No 2194 of 1941, and Hunslet (for Ruston Hornsby), No 3116 of 1944. There is now no on-site quarrying, although ground lime is produced from imported limestone, and there is also some brickmaking.

An economy of 1938, believed effective from 20 June, was the formal abandonment of Redhills Junction, the closing of the signal box there and the conversion to single track between Blencow and the Redhills Junction site. The Up and Down platforms and platform lines, as well as the Up loop, were retained at Blencow, which thus became (for the first time) a crossing place on a single line, the token section eastward extending to Penrith No 1 box.

Blencow closed to goods wef 1 June 1964, and on Monday 28 June 1965 the refuge siding, dock siding and other down yard facilities were taken out of use. However, from Monday 4 December 1967 the Down refuge siding was restored, this probably being the trail-back down the bank created in 1938 from part of the former Down running line, of 1901-38. Also from the same day 'one engine' working was introduced between Keswick and Penrith No 1 box, with a ground frame taking over the connection trailing from the former Down platform line to the Lime Company's siding. Stops were installed on the former Down line west of the platforms, and all passenger trains thereafter used the former Up platform; the signal box was closed. The station was unstaffed from 1 July 1968 and closed to passengers wef 6 March 1972, but the line itself and the quarry connections both here and at Flusco survived until final abandonment wef 19 June 1972. Blencow passenger station had earlier closed as such wef 3 March 1952, but re-opened from 2 July 1956, to survive as seen until 6 March 1972.

A pair of neat houses, gabled and with very good gardens, were built by the CKPR in 1908 near Blencow station, facing the road. A signalman occupied one and the permanent way ganger in charge from Blencow westward the other, as recalled from the 1920s-1930s. They are still smart at the time of writing.

A renowned 'character' at Blencow over many years was station master George Gaskarth, here from circa 1917 until retirement circa 1942. He had also been the parcels clerk at Cockermouth in 1913. He liked to wear his Scots regalia and march up and down Blencow platform playing his bagpipes! He was an energetic figure; after Redhills box closed in 1938 he would cheerfully walk the line down to Penrith No 1 to initiate pilot working. The romantic aura surrounding George Gaskarth diverts attention from his predecessors, who included Henry Sutcliffe (there at the start in 1865), Thomas Kidson (promoted from Blencow to station master at Keswick in April 1869), John Tinnion (moving, as already noted, to Penruddock in January 1872), John Scott (here 1872-85, then resigning), and James Hutchinson (appointed 1885 and still here in 1908, when he was offered Bassenthwaite Lake, but was left undisturbed at Blencow at his own request).

An imposing portrait of station master George Gaskarth, in charge at Blencow circa 1917-1942. He would walk the platform playing his bagpipes! *Syd Ridley collection*

Jim Airey, who had been station master at Bassenthwaite Lake, came to Blencow in the years 1964-66 as its last station master. He and Mrs Airey had happy memories of their days at both these attractive stations. Mr Edwin Thompson and Mrs Thompson, both with earlier assignments at Embleton station and level crossing – and Edwin Thompson also as signalman at Bassenthwaite Lake – made a move to Blencow in April 1966, when the railway closed west of Keswick, and took over the station house. Mr Thompson was in the box until it closed late in 1967. He and his wife continued to reside at Blencow and made progressive improvements, which since 1972 included expansion over the trackbed and platforms, forming a garden of CKPR memories, with a superb vista towards Carlisle and also the Northern Pennines.

Back in 1913 the signalman was Fred Bewley; he lived for long in LNWR Redhills Terrace, the house at the Penrith end, and died in 1956. Adam Watson was Fred's part-time relief. Alfred Ousby was a pre-1923 CKPR man who had been in Redhills box until circa 1935. He was pleasantly recalled as the Blencow signalman by Geoffrey Holt, who came to Penrith in 1945 as signalmen's Inspector. Teddy Foster knew Blencow box very well, from 1938. Tom Jackson of Keswick was a regular signalman here from about 1938 until 1967, with a background of experience as 'box lad' at Penrith No 1 in 1929, as well as at Tebay, Kirkby Lonsdale, Threlkeld and Penruddock, and subsequently having a roaming commission in the years 1967-69, between Penrith and Keswick, in the days of unmanned stations.

Blencow to Redhills Junction

The new line of 1901 was the Down road of 1901-38. From 1938 to 1972 the original line (the Up road of 1901-38) was retained for Up and Down running. A train's length of the former Down line was retained at Blencow in order to be available as a refuge for stabling Blencowe Limeworks traffic. The bank was on a down grade of 1 in 70, unbroken past Redhills, to finish at 1 in 79 near Penrith No 1 box.

7. Redhills Junction and Penrith

Redhills Junction and the NER link

Under-line bridge No 13 (Stainton Road) immediately preceded Redhills Junction. The signal box was on the right, opposite the divergence to the left of the line built by the NER, which immediately became double for the remainder of its length of rather less than 1 mile, passing under the CKPR to its convergence with the West Coast Main Line (WCML) at Eamont Junction. This was the 'Penrith Loop' or 'Redhills Curve' and descended at 1 in 66, 1 in 50 and 1 in 131, in that sequence.

At a Euston meeting in March 1864, with William Bouch representing the S&DR (strictly, by then, the NER), the junctions to be formed were styled Stainton and Yanwath (eventually Redhills and Eamont) and interim arrangements were discussed for handling mineral traffic from Durham and the Eden Valley Railway (opened 1862-63 as part of the S&DR) by way of Penrith until the 'Loop' was commissioned. This NER double line was constructed by 1865 but not yet connected at Redhills when, in May of that year, the CKPR insisted on seeing the NER's plans for the junction. The junction opened on 5 September 1866, but some residual contention about the precise layout was apparent between October 1867 and January

Redhills Junction was created in 1866 by the Stockton & Darlington Railway (later NER/LNER). Looking east, the LNER double track for Eamont Junction diverges left, and subsequently passes beneath the CKPR to descend to the WCML (see below). Its protecting Down Home signal is of CKPR type. The old signal box, which lasted until 1938, is of uncertain antecedents. The pair of railway houses are also seen. Ahead, the CKPR route, single track, descends to Penrith. *Richard L. Pattinson/CRA*

Looking north from Eamont Junction signal box in 1934, the double-track route to Redhills Junction diverges from the WCML to the left. A 'Royal Scot' three-cylinder 4-6-0 is literally roaring up the bank, southbound. *Syd Ridley*

1868. The NER recorded that the junction signal box as opened in 1866, at its expense. However, on 2 April 1890 the CKPR agreed to erect a new cabin here, as the existing frame was 'so dilapidated'. The somewhat plain and fairly tall signal box, with hipped roof, had the air of a Saxby & Farmer cabin of approximately 1870. Perhaps it was in essence the original cabin of the 1860s, retained in 1890 and equipped with a new frame by (probably) Tweedy of Carlisle. It lasted in operation until 1938.

The 'loop' was traversed by the coke trains from 1866 until, after a period of intermittent running, a last working on 18 February 1926 (C. R. Clinker's date). Excursion trains from the NER to Keswick and back used it extensively, especially between the 1890s and 1914. The LMS also used it, for circular tour trains in the 1920s, and a southbound train, remembered as being in August 1929, would probably be the last example. In 1930 the LMS Chief Signal & Telegraph Engineer paid a visit and was very disturbed by the poor, indeed unsafe condition of the 'Loop'. Some immediate work was done, but its use was

virtually restricted to the turning of the LNER 4-4-0 locomotives of 'D3' (ex-GNR) type during the years 1930-35 and, latterly, LMS former MR Class '2' 4-4-0s – all these engines being too long for Penrith's turntable. Derailment of one or more of the LNER locomotives was reported during these turning operations on the 'Loop.'

The line was condemned about 1936-37 and lifted in the period 1937-38. An official closing date was 11 June 1938 (Saturday), thus wef 13 June. Eamont Junction signal box closed wef 11 July 1938 and, as already noted, Redhills box seemingly closed wef 20 June 1938.

Redhills its people
Following receipt by the CKPR Board of a memorial from residents of nearby Stainton, it was agreed in 1871 to provide a siding at Redhills Junction for goods and mineral traffic. Nevertheless, by May 1874 the siding and its points were to be abandoned; the Board of Trade was demanding expensive alterations, having presumably awakened to the hazards of shunting on the gradient here,

with two convergences to a main line 'just down the hill'!

The two cottages adjoining the signal box were also erected under a CKPR decision of 1871 and were intended for a signalman and a platelayer. In the 1920s and 1930s each was occupied by a signalman and his family. They were rapidly becoming derelict in early 1985.

Although Redhills was a NER junction, the CKPR employed the signalmen. In January 1872 John Scott was transferred from Redhills Junction to Blencow. Edmund Porter succeeded him, but resigned in February 1873. It is implied that he would not endure the prevailing hours of duty, for in February 1873 the Board minuted that 'the signalman (clearly only one) has long hours. In future, he is to be relieved two days each week and every third Sunday by a platelayer of the Redhills length.' In July 1913 there were two full-time signalmen, J. S. Codling (who held this post from circa 1878 and died on 22 October 1916) and John Laycock. They each worked turns of 8 hours one week and 8¼ hours the next week (alternating), thus suggesting that the box was open 16¼ hours daily. Incidentally, there had been times of pressure in the iron industry when the coke trains ran over the CKPR by night, as well as during a long day. Adam Watson and Alfred Ousby (the latter later of Blencow) were the signalmen in the 1920s and 1930s and Joseph Watson joined his father, circa 1935-38.

The NER and LNER for long employed two men (a ganger and assistant) on maintenance of their double-track 'Curve', the men living just south of Redhills Junction but not in railway houses.

Redhills Junction to Penrith No 1

The NER 'Loop' or 'Curve' was crossed by the CKPR's single track by bridge No 134, known to the NER as bridge No 4; it was infilled during 1939. Onward, the four LNWR cottages of Eamont Terrace were visible (and still are) across a field and main road; they stand with the NER road bridge (now south abutment only) to one side, and the WCML (Lancaster & Carlisle Railway of old) with its Down loops (now one loop) behind them. Hereabouts, from the CKPR in fair weather,

Cross Fell, premier summit in the Pennines, can be seen ahead.

Bridge No 135 (Mile End) crossed a by-road, which has become busy since the A66 was redeveloped, and this bridge was destroyed in 1983, its abutments replaced by landscaping. 'Redhills Cottages', a terrace of eight houses backing towards the CKPR, were a casualty of the A66 roadworks.

We now complete our leisurely travels – and digressions – from Workington, Cockermouth, Keswick and many another place to descend beside the WCML and the southern approaches to Penrith.

Excitements on the bank

The runaway from Blencow to Penrith No 1 box on 26 December 1889 is described in more detail in the second volume, but there were 'happenings' in later years too.

When the long section was made between Blencow and Penrith No 1 box in 1938, the risk of accident was clearly in mind. Near MP28¼ a short portion of the old Down road was left in situ, with spring-controlled points normally set to divert a descending vehicle or train on to it and thence into a sand-drag. In order that a properly authorised descending train would not be diverted to the drag, the signalman at Blencow had first to secure the token for the section, then pull a lever that not only electrically set the catch points for safe downhill running, but also proved them set and locked before the train could be signalled down the bank.

Notwithstanding these safeguards, there was an occasion when a goods train descending from Blencow to Penrith, with the driver duly in possession of the key token, was put through the catch points on to the 'old road', heading for the sand-drag. It happened that the driver on duty that day was a cautious man – and not his 'high speed' colleague who often worked the turn – and he succeeded in stopping with minimum damage. It was never satisfactorily established how the Blencow signalman contrived to achieve this mis-setting of the catch points. He always insisted that a lightning storm at the time had upset the point motor so that the spring opened the turn-out.

Above A general view of the CKPR junction with the West Coast Main Line, viewed from Penrith No 1 signal box. Rebuilt 'Baby Scot' 4-6-0 No 45527 *Southport* passes with the lightweight two-wagon Harrison's shunt, from near Shap. The picture was taken on 31 July 1964. *Derek Cross*

Right Descending the CKPR route to Penrith No 1 (Keswick Junction) signal box, seen in the middle distance, this handsome LNWR bracket signal offered alternatives of proceeding by the CKPR line (left), 'EV line' (Eden Valley – middle), or on to the Down main line. The ground signal would indicate a road set across to the Up main and so to Penrith yard or warehouse. 15 August 1950. *E. S. Russell*

On another occasion Tom Jackson was in the box, with the road set and authorised for a goods train from Flusco to run via the loop, behind the Up platform, bound down the bank for Penrith. The driver's 'pop' whistles alerted him to a 'runaway'. The 'Black 5' 4-6-0 locomotive had left Flusco with a massive train of 40 loads of limestone products, but with no brake-van attached. The train ran by at speed – of course without picking up the token for the single line and with the driver and his mate preparing to jump off the locomotive. It just about negotiated the outlet from loop to running line and the crew stayed aboard. Tom knew that no ascending train would be due at Penrith No 1 and reckoned that if he opened the electric catch points the inevitable pile-up at the sand-drag would be on such a massive scale as to 'stop the job' for some days. He therefore sent 'Train running away' on the bell to Penrith No 1 box.

His colleague there was noted for a propensity to argue points, and so it was on this occasion, but he was given no option – the runaway was coming! As it happened, the brakes on the engine and the tender began to take effect and the train came to a stand some 2 miles down the bank from Blencow, near Redhills and still about three-quarters of a mile from the junction at Penrith. Mr Jackson's judgment was commended by higher authority.

When Blencow box closed in December 1967, and 'one engine' working applied, it was necessary to take out the electric points and sand-drag of 1938, but electrically operated points (leading to a sand-drag on the Up side) were installed only 475 yards short of, and controlled by, Penrith No 1 box, which by then had a track circuit on the branch near the new catch points. One Good Friday, after dark in the evening, the signalman was astounded and alarmed to see the track circuit light come on, indicating the approach of a train from Keswick – which was closed that day, with no known traffic. He raised the alarm and investigation was urgently set in motion, but nothing was ever found.

The CKPR approach to Penrith

Penrith station, on its sweeping curve, opened in 1846 as part of the Lancaster & Carlisle Railway, and by early 1848 it was on the first through railway route from London (Euston) to Glasgow and Edinburgh. The L&CR was leased to the LNWR in 1859 and vested in that Company in 1879, and – like the CKPR – became part of the LMS from 1923, and subsequently BR from 1948. The Eden Valley Railway (EVR) with running powers over the few miles from Eden Valley Junction (Clifton) to Penrith, fully opened in 1863, thus bringing the S&DR (soon to be the NER) and later the LNER to Penrith. The CKPR opening, it may be recalled, was in late 1864 (minerals) and January 1865 (passengers).

The Penrith Joint Station Committee was established under an Act of 1862 and its inaugural meeting was held in Penrith on 24 July 1863, with powerful representation, namely:

An evocative view of the WCML platforms at Penrith station, looking south in 1925. Note the variety of trunks, suitcases and baskets awaiting collection by a Down train. *Real Photographs Company/Courtesy Ian Allan Ltd*

LNWR: Richard Moon (Chairman); W. N. Hodgson (LNWR Director with special concern for the L&C district, and a member of the CKPR Board); William Cawkwell (General Manager); S. B. Worthington (Engineer).

S&DR (strictly, **NER**): John Whitwell; Thomas MacNay (Secretary of the former S&DR); Johnathan Dixon.

CKPR: Isaac Fletcher (Vice Chairman); Isaac Lowthian (Director); John Wood (then Resident Engineer on construction, under Thomas Bouch); Henry Cattle (Secretary and Manager).

Improvements at Penrith were planned and put in hand, and followed up at the ensuing meeting, at Euston, on 16 March 1864 in anticipation of opening of the CKPR.

The Keswick line was provided with an entry to Penrith parallel with, but independent of, the LNWR main lines, so that CKPR passenger trains could run without hindrance to the back face of the Down platform. The NER secured its 'EVR bay' in the south end of that platform. This remained, broadly, the layout right through the years until the EVR passenger services ceased in 1962 and those from Keswick in 1972. Strictly, the EVR trains had an approach line of their own in due course.

More contentious were the arrangements for a running connection between the Keswick line and the main lines at the point where the routes came alongside one another, well to the south of the station. When Captain Rich, RE (for the Board of Trade) gave approval on 22 December 1864 to the opening of the CKPR to passengers, he emphasised that the junction with the main line lacked adequate signalling and interlocking and must not be used by passenger trains. In particular, the Captain disapproved of 'the two semaphores which control the CKPR's junction with the Up

An interesting scene at 'Penrith for Ullswater Lake' on 13 August 1950. The Summer Sundays-only evening train (note the express train headlamp code) is ready to leave the 'CKP' platform, bound for Darlington via Stainmore. The double-heading suggests a heavy train, which was probably too long to be accommodated at the NER bay (seen on the right). LNER (NER) Class 'J21' 0-6-0s Nos 65100 and 65038 are in charge. The track running to the left of the train shed was the CKPR run-round loop. *Neville Fields*

main line of the LNWR: one is at the junction signalman's box and one at the opposite side of the line, near the end of the branch.' The box was a pointsman's cabin on the Up (southbound) side of all tracks, fairly handy for access to the cattle sidings and the crossover between Up main and Keswick line, but remote from the signal for the protection of the junction against trains approaching from the Keswick line, on its descending grade. It took some 15 more years to achieve signalling at Penrith that gained Board of Trade approval and stood the test of time – right down to the coming of centralised power signalling in 1973.

Developments and improvements at Penrith station in the period 1865-1922 were normally on LNWR initiative and implemented according to that Company's own plans and designs. The other Companies were consulted chiefly to obtain their often reluctant contributions to the cost. Some examples:

February 1870: A scheme estimated at £1,120 for the concentrated control of points and signals was trimmed to one costed at £100 for connecting four pairs of points to the existing 'raised signal box at the south end of the station … to obviate the signalman going down to hold them'. So far as one can judge, this was the box referred to in 1864, or one shown on early maps a little to its north, also on the Up side of the main line. (Penrith No 3 box, by Saxby & Farmer, was built at the north end of the station in 1872, acquiring a replacement LNWR frame of 23 levers in 1884.)

February 1876: The LNWR secured approval of £1,371 expenditure for the construction of a signal box 'at the west end of the passenger station, to work the points and signals in that part'. One is forced to conclude that the resultant signal box was Penrith No 2, located just south of the station, on the Down side near the turntable, and surviving to be rebuilt in 1950 and closed in 1968.

Ivatt 'Mickey Mouse' 2-6-0 No 46491 drifts past Penrith No 1 box with six maroon-liveried LMS coaches comprising a Keswick-Manchester train of 18 August 1962. This view shows the track layout in the vicinity of the signal box, and the CKPR connections to the WCML and the EV line. *Derek Cross*

November 1878-February 1879: Discussion over this period produced approval of the LNWR plan, which was designed to meet BOT requirements, 'for removal of the signal cabin from the proximity of the Up shunting siding to the Down side of the line, with locking of facing points and renewal and remodelling of signals for Penrith Junction and Station'; the estimate was £1,330. In August 1880 the work was reported recently completed. The new box, on the Down side, would be 'Penrith No 1 – Keswick Junction', 1 mile 418 yards from Redhills Junction and 638 yards short of Penrith station. It was of standard LNWR pre-1903 type, with 64 levers, and lasted until 1973, signalling every Keswick line train in and out of Penrith from 1880 until 1972. The box replaced in 1879-80 is thought to have been by Saxby & Farmer, dating from circa 1872 and itself replacing the pointsman's cabin mentioned in 1864 (cf also the alterations that had been contemplated in 1870).

Other station improvements at Penrith

During the years 1866-72 various adjustments were made relating to the main Up platform, and the station staff were provided with rather more accommodation. A passenger subway under the main-line tracks was put in hand in 1872. On the Down side, a request of the NER was met in 1875 by extending the platform at the south end so that their passengers would not have to board summer trains from ground level. Meanwhile, in December 1867, the LNWR were installing a boiler for hot water for carriage footwarmers, the cost of this too being for joint account. The CKPR back platform road was snug but somewhat gloomy; it had the advantage of a through track, so that trains from Keswick could call there, then proceed to Carlisle.

Goods and coal at Penrith

There had been a contract for local cartage with Mr Dennison, but it was found

At Penrith's Up main line platform, LMS No 5068 *Miranda* (a 'Jumbo' 2-4-0) and a 'Cauliflower' 0-6-0 are doubtless working a through train from Glasgow or Carlisle to Keswick. Note the distinctive water tower at the southern end of the Up platform. *Howard Vogt collection/courtesy Preston Whiteley*

unsatisfactory and from October 1879 the LNWR employed four horses of their own. Much later, in December 1914, six horses were stabled at Penrith yard, four employed on NER goods cartage and two on 'joint cartage'. The LNWR were providing new stables at that time. The Railway layout and buildings in the yard were elaborated in detail from time to time.

Coal was handled on a substantial scale and at one time the coal agent was Robert Pearson, not a Company or Joint employee. He considered the local station master's agency at Blencow station to represent unfair competition, but the CKPR Board did not agree. In 1908 he addressed letters to individual Directors of the Keswick Company about 'coal sales by the station masters at roadside stations', but he was rebuffed. Note that on the CKPR line, most station yards were provided with coal depots from early days. From 1 January 1869 the rent for coal vaults (coal cells) at stations was to cease and in future 3d per ton was to be charged on all coal sold from the station depots and 1d per ton for all coal weighed by the Company's machine. This appeared to relate the fees paid by coal merchants (including, presumably, station masters in some instances) to the turnover of their businesses.

After the once busy goods yard at Penrith closed, wef 7 January 1971, a rail-served coal concentration depot remained on part of the site, but this ceased to receive its deliveries by rail within a very few years.

Penrith engine shed

It was evident that the stabling of locomotives at Penrith to work, or share the working, of the CKPR line would be desirable. The subject was mentioned briefly in the first station agreement (24 April 1861) and more specifically in the fourth clause of the second agreement (11 September 1862). With the opening of the line imminent, the subject was raised at Euston during the meeting of 14 July 1864. Mr Hoskins, the CKPR Chairman, held that clause four of 1862 contemplated the CKPR providing steam sheds on its own line (one presumes for use by LNWR locomotives

working CKPR traffic), but LNWR Chairman Richard Moon did not agree. Rather amusingly, David and Goliath appointed an arbitrator: Christopher Johnstone, General Manager of the Caledonian Railway, of the evocative address '302 Buchanan Street, Glasgow'. His handling of the reference was so delicate that he failed to clarify between the alternatives:

1. The LNWR are to build engine sheds, with the CKPR paying rent for the exclusive use of the premises; or
2. The CKPR are to build the sheds, for the free use of LNWR locomotives employed on the CKPR line.

He nevertheless appeared to show that the CKPR had some such obligation as outlined in Option No 2. Mr Hodgson, a Director of both the LNWR and CKPR, suggested that the understanding was that the LNWR should build the shed at Penrith, 'adjoining the engine turntable', the CKPR paying into the joint fund a rent for the land but the LNWR paying proportionately if the shed was used to some extent for its own purposes. In fact (September 1864), the LNWR expressed the intention of building the shed forthwith, with the CKPR paying interest at 6% on the outlay, with adjustment if the shed were used other than for solely CKPR purposes. This was agreed.

The shed was duly built by the LNWR – in 1865, it has been understood, but correspondence of 1869 implies that it was only in use from 1 July 1868. The Keswick Company protested strongly that it had been led to expect a cost of £600, but was being asked (in January 1869) to pay more than five times this sum. The LNWR evidently resubmitted the actual cost at £1,440 and a compromise was then agreed, whereby the CKPR would pay interest on a notional £1,000, this arrangement to take account of some use of the shed by LNWR engines not wholly engaged on the CKPR line. Down the years Penrith engines and men had daily duties to and from Carlisle with local passenger trains.

The S&DR/NER also had certain rights

in the matter of a locomotive shed, dating from around 1865, and when they applied for use of its facilities in 1866 numerous excuses were received (from the LNWR?) and no accommodation was forthcoming. In February 1871 Mr Mackay wrote to the Keswick management asking for extension of the Penrith engine shed to permit stabling of one of their engines and to obviate its running through to Kirkby Stephen. The reply was that the CKPR did not propose to expend money on the LNWR premises, but would consider favourably providing CKPR land on which the NER might build a shed. The NER did not let the matter drop and the emphasis shifted, to a financial arrangement. In February 1873 it was agreed (and minuted by the CKPR) that the Keswick Company allow £25 per annum to 'the S&D Company' in lieu of providing accommodation at Penrith for one of its engines working over the CKPR line, the allowance to apply from the time when the accommodation became available. The arithmetic emerges from NER records as:

The LNWR extended its Penrith shed, following NER pressure, at the cost of £750
- on which sum the CKPR
  agreed to pay its usual 6%   £45 pa
- but with the NER contributing
  to this sum   £20 pa
- and the CKPR therefore
  having a net outgoing of   £25 pa

There remains an element of mystery. So far as is known, the requirement of the NER (and LNER) was always to stable overnight a single passenger engine that had worked its last Down train in the evening and would work the early Up departure for the EVR line, until this stabling ceased in the summer of 1939. It is unclear why the CKPR should contribute, as the NER loco was not one engaged in mineral workings over the route to Cockermouth.

The need for the engine shed at Penrith was much reduced after diesel railcars took over most passenger duties on the Keswick road in 1955, with Carlisle (Upperby) and Workington depots providing such steam power as was necessary, and the odd contribution from Oxenholme. The shed at Penrith therefore closed wef 18 June 1962.

* * *

The railway route through northern Lakeland, from Penrith to Workington, was founded on the demands of industry, so this history continues in the second volume with the fascinating tale of the mineral and freight traffics, before moving on to consider passenger traffic, which only developed to its peak as the iron and steel-based movements declined and largely disappeared.

As this volume started at the western end of the line in Workington station, so we bring our leisurely journey to a close in the Down main line platform at Penrith. LNWR 'Cauliflower' 0-6-0s Nos 58396 and 28555 are seen at rest after arriving with the 8.35am from Workington on 16 July 1949. Note the water tower, similar to that provided at the southern end of the Up platform. *J. D. Darby*

Acknowledgements and sources

It has been a pleasure and privilege to enjoy the co-operation of many old and new friends in the course of my research and in furthering the presentation of the story of the cross-country railway through Lakeland. The archives staff at Carlisle Castle have been ever-patient and the WCML has become well-worn in the course of 'day trips' of more than 500 miles between Oxenholme and Kew Gardens, for delvings in the Public Record Office. Above all, I thank the many folk who devoted their working lives to the railway concerned, or lived and maybe farmed beside it and then talked with me; clarity of recollection provides a wonderful perspective for the historian. I thank, among others:

Jim Airey and Mrs Airey, Frank Alcock, Roy Anderson, Doctor Michael Andrews, G. J. Aston, Nancy Banks-Smith, Mrs Bennett, J. S. Berry, Ian Bishop (and Trust House Forte, for whom he is a manager), Robert Bond, George Bott, Alan Bottomley, W. E. Boyd, J. Bernard Bradbury, Henry and Mrs Briggs, Derek J. W. Brough, Joe W. Brownrigg, Dorothy Butcher, Ian S. Carr, Joseph C. Carruthers and Mrs Elizabeth Carruthers (nee Longcake), Oliver F. Carter, John McG. Charters, Les G. Charlton, Frank Clarkson, J. G. Coates, Edgar Corless, Elizabeth Cook, Mary Cowperthwaite, Bert and Mrs Cowperthwaite, Derek Cross, E. Lloyd Daniels (and the Derwent Railway Society), J. D. Darby, W. B. Darnell, John Dawson, Alan G. Dunbar, John Duncan, Hugh G. Ellison, John Farrer, Gordon and Mrs Ferries, Neville Fields, Edward Foster, Richard D. Foster, E. H. Fowkes, Gregory R. Fox, Mrs. Emily Gates, Gordon Graham, Jack Hall, John M. Hammond, Eric W. Hannan, Kenneth Harper, Stanley and Mrs Harrison, Tom W. Hartley, William and Mrs Hebson, Major J. W. B. Hext, J. D. Hinde, Robert Hodgson, Peter Holmes, Geoffrey O. Holt, Kenneth Hoole, Geoffrey Horsman, Philip Houldershaw, the Reverend Rodney Hughes, Roy V. Hughes MBE, T. A. Hughes, Harry Jack, Tom W. Jackson and Mrs Jackson, David Jenkinson, Mrs Mary Johnston, William and Mrs Kelt, Jack Y. Lancaster, Robert Leslie, Lance Laverick, Geoffrey Lord, Peter and Ann Los, John McCallum, R. B. Hasell McCosh, Gurney MacInnes, John Mandale, Thomas Murray, Charles Neele, Edwin K. Nelson, Gordon Nichol, Kenneth J. Norman, Cecil and Mrs Oldfield, Barbara M. Patterson, John and Mrs Pattinson, Clive Pattinson, Derek A. Pattinson, George H. Pattinson, Michael Peascod, J. D. Petty, Ronald N. Redman, Syd and Mrs Ridley, John E. Roberts, Peter W. Robinson, Miss Mary Routledge, Eric S. Russell, Ian G. Sadler, Percy and Mrs Sanderson, Carol Sarsfield-Hall, Mr and Mrs Scott, James L. Slater, David L. Smith, H. R. Stones, D. H. Stuart, Ted Talbot, Richard Tangye, Thomas Taylor, David F. Tee, Albert Tims, John Tinkler, Thomas Tinkler, Joseph and Mrs Tinnion, Ron Tinnion, Jessie Titterington, Edwin and Marina Thompson, Oswald W. Todhunter, Jack Tyson, Phoebe Wallace, A. StG. Walsh, Edward Watson, Joseph K. Watson, Joseph Watson (of Workington), D. R. Wattleworth, David R. Webb, G. D. Whitworth, James Willan, J. Banks Wivell and Mrs Wivell (nee Philipson), Bob Wren, William Young and Mrs Young (formerly Hughes).

Special thanks are due to Arthur Chambers for his encouragement, and various cartography; to Doug Rendell for his extensive and professional photographic copying and other work on my behalf; and to Ken Norman for his enthusiastic pilotage in the Richard Pattinson collection (which is in the care of the Cumbrian Railways Association). Photographers and sources of illustrations are acknowledged individually, where known to me. Friends who have read critically and most helpfully through drafts of various parts of the work are: Richard Foster, John Hammond, Kenneth Hoole, Roy Hughes, David Tee, Albert Tims and Dudley Whitworth.

Authorities consulted include the Public Record Office, Kew; the National Railway Museum Library, York (with a special word of thanks for John Edgington); the Cumbria County Record Office, Carlisle Castle (Bruce Jones and colleagues); Abbot Hall Art Gallery and Museum, Kendal (Miss Mary Burkitt and colleagues); the Fitz Museum, Keswick (Norman Gandy); Manchester Central Library (and notably Harry Horton); Tullie House Library, Carlisle (Mr Wilkinson and Mr White); the library of the Institution of Civil Engineers; Cumbria County Council (Bridges Department); the Keswick Convention (Maurice Rowlandson and colleagues); British Railways (several departments, including Robert H. Blyth and colleagues of Manchester, on signalling; the Chief Civil Engineer, LMR, and his colleagues at Preston; and Messrs Nicholson and Copeland at Workington); and John Hurst and colleagues at the *Cumberland & Westmorland Herald*, Penrith, who also readily offered the hospitality of their archives.

Works of reference

The Iron and Steel Industry of West Cumberland J. Y. Lancaster & D. R. Wattleworth, 1977

Railway Reminiscences G. P. Neele, 1904

A History of the Cockermouth, Keswick and Penrith Railway W. McGowan Gradon, 1948

The Cockermouth, Keswick and Penrith Railway – In Memoriam J. M. Hammond, 1972

Forgotten Railways of North West England John Marshall, 1981

A Regional History of the Railways: the Lake Counties David Joy, 1983

The North Eastern Railway W. W. Tomlinson, 1914

The Stainmore Railway K. Hoole, 1973

History of Cockermouth J. Bernard Bradbury

Threlkeld, Cumbria; Glimpses of Village History J. H. Vine Hall, Threlkeld, 1977

Diary of George Schollick, 1893-1928

The Chronicles of Boulton's Siding Alfred Rosling Bennett, 1927, ref pp46-47 and 264

Cumbrian Families and Heraldry Roy Huddleston & R. S. Boumphrey

Notable Cumbrians Chance

Westmorland and Cumberland Leaders Ernest Gaskell

The Impact of the Railway on the development of Keswick as a tourist resort, 1860-1914 Dissertation by Paul Richard McGloin, University of Lancaster

Register of Closed Passenger and Goods Stations C. R. Clinker, 1978, and supplements

A Biographical Dictionary of Railway Engineers John Marshall, 1978

The Railway Magazine, 1897-1984, in particular 1907 (first part), J. Thornton Burge on pp372-373; and 1921 (second part), Cecil J. Allen on pp73-80

Trains Illustrated, year 1961, Cecil J. Allen on pp598-604 & 629

Cumbria December, 1966 pp432-5 and February 1973 (W. R. Mitchell on Threlkeld)

Newsletter of the Cumbrian Railways Association, including E. Craven on locomotives of the C&WR in February 1978 p9 and October 1978 pp2-5; P. W. Robinson on the CK&PR until 1866, in July 1979 pp5-7; G. Thomlinson on early days, in August 1984 pp41-46

Newsletter of the National Trust, on Canon Rawnsley

Journal of the Stephenson Locomotive Society, especially on LNWR engine sheds, and J. W. Armstrong on Tebay (the latter in 1953, pp161-2)

The Railway Observer (RCTS), particularly in the later 1930s and subsequently on renumbering of motive power depots

Railway Junction Diagrams (of the Railway Clearing House)

Ordnance Survey map sheets to 25-inch scale, various editions

Bradshaw's Railway Timetables and *Bradshaw's Manual*, various years

Index